Watering the Roots

Watering the Roots

A 1-2-3 Parent Wellbeing Guide
(a Muslim Perspective)

Aminah Chao Mah

The events and conversations in this book have been set down to the best of the author's ability, although some names and details may have been changed to protect the privacy of individuals.

Copyright © 2021 by Aminah Mah

All rights reserved. No part of this book may be reproduced or used in any manner without written permission of the copyright owner except for the use of quotations in a book review. For more information, address: info@dewtiful.com.au.

First paperback edition July 2021
First ebook edtion 2021
First audiobook edition 2023

Book cover art by Dr. Evelyn Bach
Photography by Sales Mohamad
Book design by Sarco Press

ISBN 978-0-646-83470-2 (paperback)

www.dewtiful.com.au

Dedication

I dedicate this book to all parents who strive to arrive at their final destination with a tranquil heart.

Contents

Foreword ix
Acknowledgments xi
Greetings to the Reader xiii

Chapter One: Parenteering—A Mindset 1
Chapter Two: Parenting For Ultimate Wellbeing—
A Perspective 19
Chapter Three: Wellbeing Guide First Component:
One-Way Journey Home 39
Chapter Four: Wellbeing Guide Second Component:
Two-Fold, Double-Selection 53
Chapter Five: Wellbeing Guide Third Component: 69
Chapter Six: Inward Connection 81
Chapter Seven: Vertical Connection 131
Chapter Eight: Outward/External Connection ... 167
Chapter Nine: Applying The 1-2-3 Wellbeing Guide 205
Chapter Ten: Go The Extra Mile 231

Glossary of Terms 255
References 261
About the Author 283

Foreword

ALL PRAISES ARE due to the Al-Mighty Allah and sincere prayers of peace upon His final Messenger, Muhammad, his noble companions and companions.

Dr Aminah Chao Mah, author of *Watering the Roots: A 1-2-3 Parent Wellbeing Guide (a Muslim Perspective)* is a colleague with years of professional and practical lived life experience watering roots of many children—her own and countless others.

I truly enjoyed, benefitted and resonated with the themes, methodology and systems discussed in this dissertation. Parenteering, as Dr Mah champions, is not an exact science and is not a one size fits all for all families, circumstances and cultures. This text, however, does not presume that it is the magic bullet to end all strain. It is a measured and articulate presumption that the more you invest in your children—time, wealth, discipline, learning, candour and most importantly, Love, and you will have achieved success in putting them on the right path.

This book is theologically sound as per the dictates of the Sunni tradition of Islam and it is consistent with the greater aims of the Sunnah—methodology—of the noble Prophet Muhammad, peace be upon him.

By virtue of my experience and study, I recommend this book to you and pray that it reaches the east and the west. Both will benefit from it in differing, albeit, complimentary ways.

Imam Yahya Ibrahim
A/Principal
Al-Ameen College
Islamic Chaplain—Curtin University
& University of Western Australia

Acknowledgments

ALL PRAISES ARE due to my Creator, the Lord of the worlds.

This book is a humble attempt at summing up the many years of learning and growth of my very imperfect but real human experience as a parent. I have learnt from innumerable teachers, formal and informal, whom I am thankful for.

Much of who I am I owe it to my parents. I will never be able to repay you for the sacrifice and love you gave me. May Allah reward you both for the strong values and principles you modelled to me and grant you the highest level of Paradise. Please remember to ask for me when you are rewarded with your final abode of bliss so I may reunite with you by Allah's Grace.

To Dr Eltaiba, Dr Yucel, Imam Yahya, Sister Zalina and Sister Aisha, may Allah reward you for reading the initial manuscript and for your generous constructive criticism that helped me to improve on it.

To Rebecca, I could not have done it without your sound advice and meticulous editing. To Raihanaty, thank you for sharing your experience and the tips you gave me that kept me going at times when I felt like giving up. As my PA in the publication process, your step-by-step guidance has been indispensable.

To all who inspired me to improve as a person, who cheered me on along the way, may you continue to teach me, correct me and support me.

To Abdullah, my co-captain on our parenting journey, thank you for always believing in me more than I believe in myself. Your patience and encouragement healed my insecurities. Your questions had an invaluable influence on the way I shaped my thoughts for this book.

I cannot write as a parent had it not been for my three beloved children. You have completely changed my perspective on parenting and through you I came face to face with my inner self, the good, the bad and the ugly. To Osama, Latifa and Sakina, thank you for enriching my life.

Greetings to the Reader

Dear Reader,
Welcome to *Watering the Roots*.
Unlike the new garment we buy, children do not come with care instructions. There is no standard manual for raising children. There is no one right way, understandably so, since each and every child is unique. Each family's circumstance is different. Even identical twins differ in their personalities. We as parents chug along with whatever we know to the best of our abilities. This is not a book on parenting techniques. It is a book for you to develop wellbeing, with the hope that you model your wellbeing practices to your children.

Let me begin with a quick backstory to this book. I am a mother of three, a boy and two girls, all of whom are adults now. I had my fair share of panic, frustration, and regrets as a parent. Since I did not have any extended family around to guide me, I needed help big time. I attended many community-initiated workshops on parenting, as well as personal development courses, such as communication, goal setting, leadership, etc.

Since the early 1990s I have been blessed with opportunities to work with Muslim youth and their parents, which led me to pursue my teaching qualifications and later, higher degrees in education. My research focused on parenting and wellbeing of Muslim children in a Western context.

My study on positive psychology and wellbeing after completing my PhD prompted me to really connect with myself. I started to reflect on my own parenting approach and objective. Each time I had a lightbulb moment, I would ask: why didn't someone tell me this when I was a young parent? I eventually came to a clear goal for parenting, which is wellbeing; for parents first and foremost, but nonetheless, for our children. I feel truly blessed. To give back, I decided to put my drop in the ocean by turning my notes and thoughts into a book rooted in the core values and wellbeing practices I hold dear, to share with all parents, both Muslims and people in other faith communities.

I write under a general presumption that all parents intend for their children happiness, strong values, sound character, safety, security, adequate education and skills to earn a respectable living, good friends, and successful career, to name a few. Sometimes the weight of making these wishes a reality in our minds can be so heavy that we lose sight of why we do what we do. I hope to help parents effect a paradigm shift in their perspective on what really matters.

At the heart of my book, I present to you a 1-2-3 Wellbeing Guide. It is a guide with some interconnected concepts, constructed in an easy to remember format, so you may use it as a tool to help you fulfill your responsibilities and parental roles with relative clarity and ease.

Some of you may even resonate with my experiences of parenting with baggage that influenced many of our decisions in our children's upbringing, some of which we were not even aware until much later. I am a child of refugee parents and grandparents. Survival was our primary goal. To strive for success was not negotiable. This success included how well we did with our lives, and how well our children turned out within very limited resources. Successful parenting was vaguely defined by children with good manners, strong religious identity, who excelled in their studies that opened ways to good careers. The wellbeing of parents and children among us back then was therefore closely identified with this idea of success.

This book is useful for migrant parents who have to deal with the stress of adjusting to cultures and traditions between the old and the new, while working hard to gain acceptance in the new society. I know what juggling acts are involved, having had to compromise my own career aspirations to raising children on limited financial means without extended family support.

We lived through the war on terrorism amidst waves of hostility against Muslims on many fronts: the media, politicians and the society in which we lived. We felt our existence as Muslims in a Western society stuck out like a sore thumb. Many innocent Muslims had fallen victims to religion-based racist attacks. Parents have to stay strong and guide their children to decipher their identity through the thick fog of Islamophobia.

I had come to the realisation that the success we were after most of our lives mentioned previously, was only a by-product of the goal that really mattered. The real goal as I have come to learn, in my humble opinion, is to pursue our ultimate wellbeing in this life and in the Hereafter. The way to achieve this is through maintaining a sound and tranquil heart. Understanding this goal was not only important to me as an individual, but more so as a parent.

For this very reason, I want to share my experiences and insights with you; like me, you may at times be wishing that someone would remind you of the bigger picture when you feel stuck; or to offer a word of reassurance when you slip into momentary disillusionment and to cheer you on along this worthy and honourable journey you have been blessed with.

I hope this book enhances your and your children's wellbeing.

Aminah Chao Mah

CHAPTER ONE
Parenteering—A Mindset

Children learn more from what you are than what you teach[1]

This Occupation Called Parenting

EVERY STAGE OF a child's development poses different challenges. I am writing this book not because I think I have aced it. Quite the contrary, I am sharing what I have learnt from my innumerable stuff-ups. As harshly as I judge myself, my three children are still willing to confide in me and regularly make time to catch up with me. I guess children are more gracious than parents give them credit for.

However, I still feel my heart constrict on occasion, wishing I had done things differently.

This is because, even with over three decades of being a parent, I am still on my journey. Parenting is an endless evolution of our relationship with our children, and with ourselves.

Have you ever regretted things you did or said to your child/children? If you answered yes you must know that you and I are not the only ones feeling this way. And do you know something else? What you are experiencing is growth. Yes, growth. You are feeling what you are feeling now because you have come to learn that there is a different way, perhaps a better way to do things. Sure, you cannot undo what has already been done, but you certainly can do things differently next time now that you have learnt something else that may be more effective.

For new parents, let this book be your older companion who has traversed the same path not so long before you. Let this book add to your wellbeing development.

You, The Parenteer

I was deeply immersed in collecting and analysing the experiences of parents in my case studies on parenting Muslim children in Australia for my Master's thesis in 2008, when I made up the word *'parenteering'* in my head. I saw all of the parents I interviewed like orienteers. They had goals for their children and they were diligent like explorers using whatever tools they had to find their way.

A *parenteer* is someone who considers his/her parental role like an orienteer. An orienteer sets off with a destination/goal in mind although they have never been on the journey before. I came to the conclusion that the destination for parenteers is to arrive at a state of being—ultimate wellbeing—in this life and in the Hereafter. This state of wellbeing is all encompassing but can be pinpointed to its essence of having attained a tranquil heart. Parenteers need a good road map and compass, with which they work diligently with their children towards their destination.

Map

Parenteers need a map. A map that will help them find their way to their destination—a sound and peaceful heart. Throughout the history of humanity, our Creator has been sending down maps we call holy scriptures to different communities through hand-picked role models we call prophets and messengers of the divine. The road map I recommend my Muslim readers to refer to is the Qur'an. It is the same road map I base my key concepts on life and death and our goals in this book. Readers of other religions may resonate with many of the concepts and values discussed in this book.

Admittedly my husband and I crossed many intersections along our journey where we felt lost. We looked for signs and clues that would help us get out of our roadblocks. Having that good map has been a great help, and it continues to be. Over time, we learned to trust that even if we felt lost at certain points, following the map gave us reassurance that we could get back on track if we kept trying.

Compass

The compass for parenteers is our inbuilt ability to discern right from wrong, our gut feelings, and a sound decision-making process. Do not be defeated by errors you make along the way. Parenting always includes trials and errors that people call 'learning on the job'. We have our predecessors' successes and errors to learn from as well. Value all experiences past and present because all parents are merely parenteers.

Begin With A Growth Mindset

From the outset, this means you as a *parenteer* do not need to know it all. In truth, who does? Marisa de los Santos says this about parenting:

> No one is ever quite ready; everyone is always caught off guard. Parenthood chooses you. And you open your eyes, look at what you've got, say 'Oh, my gosh,' and recognize that of all the balls there ever were, this is the one you should not drop. It's not a question of choice.[2]

Fumbling, stumbling and feeling lost are part and parcel of parenting. I want to reassure you that whatever you have been doing, you need to acknowledge that you have done your best, and, with a growth mindset, you must believe you have the capacity to learn, and you will continue to do better. Value your experiences as building blocks you cannot do without. Acknowledge these feelings but do not dwell on them.

When you appreciate yourself a little, the job becomes more do-able. When you do away with unrealistic expectations, any progress you make becomes your strength. And you will all do better. This has been proven true in the Broaden and Build theory by Barbara Fredrickson, one of the prominent researchers in Positive Psychology in the US. Through her research, Fredrickson has found that positivity literally opens us up. Positivity expands a person's peripheral vision and the conceptual connections one makes. One notices more, comes up with more alternatives and better solutions to problems and one sees other people with new perspectives, which help them to connect with others in more positive ways.[3]

As parenteers, you are literally finding your way. When a growth mindset is applied to our parenting, we will be amazed by what a positive mind will do for us. It opens us up to learn, to care, to see and to connect with our children in an upward spiral.

Your Children As Mystery Seedlings

Consider your children as mystery seedlings. None of us knows what they are like and what they will become except the One who created them. You start off by doing the generally agreed upon things like giving them water, feeding them nutrients and putting them in a sunny and airy area. You learn to develop general caring routines for your seedlings. You wish for this to be the extent of your duty. But God knows you are capable of doing more. He gives you all kinds of trials to make *you* grow.

Challenges Expand Parenting Knowledge And Skills

You will find that while one seedling thrives in direct sunlight, another seedling is withering. You run straight to the hobby section in the library to see what you can do. You match this seedling's characteristics as best as you can with the ones in the book and come home armed with the new idea to move the seedling into a slightly shady area. A few days later you notice this seedling standing up a little straighter and you say to yourself this little seedling likes the shade. As you breathe a sigh of relief the corner of your eye catches the burnt tips on the leaves of your other seedling in the sun.

You say to yourself with confidence, *I know what to do now; I'll just move you under the pergola too*. In just a matter of days this stressed seedling puzzles you even more. Now it looks sickly. You think, oh no what have I done? What should I do now? You find the local horticulturist. She asks you to describe this seedling. She tilts her head to think for a while then she says suggestively, 'You wouldn't suppose its leaves are distressed from wind burn?' Your eyes light up. This horticulturist is a genius. Right where this seedling is planted is where you and your spouse love to sit for the beautiful breeze in that passage. Now that you think about it, it has been a little dry of late when the hot wind passes. So you go home to find something that shields the seedling from the draughty wind yet still allows the sunshine to bathe on the seedling.

On goes this process of asking, adjusting, learning, observing and tweaking to care for your mystery seedlings. You learn that each plant has their individual character, idiosyncrasies, likes, dislikes, vulnerabilities and strengths. Sometimes you feel tired from the responsibility and overwhelmed by the problems they present one after another, but you just cannot take your mind off them. They pull on your heartstrings.

Each Seedling Is Unique

Over time your seedlings grow up. One may give you beautiful flowers but you need to be careful with its thorns on the stem; another may give you delicious fruits but you need to be vigilant against the pests that also share your love for the fruits. Some may not give either, quietly growing plainly but when you gently brush over their leaves they give off such invigorating scent that keeps luring you back to touch them. Just when you think you had chosen your favourite another reveals its marvel that gives you joy beyond description. Occasionally you feel like banging your head against the brick wall over one seedling because nothing you do seems to make any difference until one day it suddenly stands green and straight as if to say, look, Mum and Dad, sorry it took me a while but here I am, all grown up! It continues to grow by centimetres rapidly into a tall, strong, delightful bamboo plant! You mutter to yourself, whoa ... to think I almost gave up...

Such is the job of parenting.

Think Parenteering Makes You Feel Lighter

In many ways all parents are like that gardener with mystery seedlings in their hands. No parent is born to know how best to care for this young living, breathing, kicking bundle in his or her arms. That is part of the challenge! You will continue to strive to do your best because 'of all the balls there ever were, this is the one you should not drop'.

And indeed, if you leave perfection out of your criteria as a parent, and treat this job with all the right intentions as a *journey of discovery* by trial and error, you may actually fly higher because you are literally lighter in your heart. This lightness is what the content of this book hopes to offer.

In this book I wish to share my experiences and those of others with my fellow parenteers, to help you nurture your children without carrying the burdens of social and self-inflicted expectations. It in no way trivialises the extent of the responsibility of parenting. The objective of this book is for you to implement the practices to nourish yourself as a person, and as a parenteer, with a hidden motive that your wellbeing practices will ripple onto your children to live a flourishing life.

Parenting In The Twenty-First Century

In all fairness parents have legitimate reasons to worry about how best to bring up their children. This occupation of parenting in the twenty-first century is challenging. It worries you how each one of your children will turn out in this increasingly complicated world. Not only are you concerned for their education, their character, their spiritual development, their physical and mental stability, you also have so many external temptations, complex moral issues and foreign ideologies to sort through in the mix.

Then there is cyberbullying which makes you feel on edge. You know well the internet has become an essential part of our modern life yet it is a double-edged sword if misused. Long gone are the days when parents kept their children at home from influences of the big bad world. You remember a time when you fought with your parents over how much television you were allowed to watch. You now wish you could turn back the clock to the days when there were only two channels, or better still, no television at all. Actually, television is no longer the big bad wolf. Thanks to wifi now your adolescent children are ALWAYS wanting to spend more time on their devices. They have access to information about absolutely anything under the sun. Every year they beg for an upgraded gadget that 'all their friends at school have'. You have nightmares about what they will be exposed to when you turn your back on them. Not only that, they want to spend more and more time on their games, and with their friends, online and offline. You cannot help but wonder what their friends are like and what they get up to when they are out of your sight. All the physical and mental stress from ensuring your child's safety perhaps make you wish for a chance to escape from it even for just a moment!

As I draw on theories of scholarly work in preparation for this book, I feel the lightness in what the word parenteering carries. It is just what every parent needs to help them get through some of those worrisome, challenging, head-butting and heart-wrenching times of raising children. As long as one has a clear destination, a solid reference to check back on, and a functional internal compass, one can hope to survive the storms. Parenteering avails parents a strip of psychological space.

If you resonate with what I am saying, this book is for you to see things with new perspectives, and to apply the recommended practices for your own wellbeing. We all need to have a clear mind to steer the ship when the seas are rough. I wish to urge you to start practising looking after your own wellbeing so that you have more to give to your children.

Parenteers, Buckle Up For The Journey!

My struggles when my children were young may be different to yours but they are struggles nonetheless. Sometimes I wish there were some mandatory pre-parental training to at least provide new parents with some baseline preparation. Fortunately there is an abundance of resources on parenting today written by experts for those who are looking for that extra bit of help. They provide a starting point for inexperienced parents. We were living in Jeddah where my husband worked in the first few years of our marriage. When we found out we were expecting our first child, we went out to the only English bookstore there was in Jeddah and came home with a copy of Dr. Spock's *Baby and Child Care*. That was in the mid-1980s. Together with my nursing background, that book helped me care for our son's physical development in those early years of parenthood.

These days many avenues have availed parents access to information, community initiatives and professional led forums on raising children more effectively. Sometimes too much information can also be confusing, if not overwhelming. What you need is to listen to your own instincts when trawling through the masses of information out there.

Now comes the time where I must break the bad news to you. No matter how much knowledge you have about parenting, I guarantee you plenty of occasions when you will be left to your own devices to figure a way out of your unique challenges. Nothing prepares you sufficiently like real life problems.

Challenges As A Migrant Parent

Let me share one of my parenting experiences with you. Just when I thought I almost survived my son's first two years, I found myself in unchartered waters after we migrated to Australia. I do not think our parents or grandparents could offer much advice on specific issues I faced as a migrant parent then.

With our toddler and a second child on the way, I had to adapt in every aspect. I juggled work, home, learning new rules, social etiquette, resources, etc., not only for myself, but also as a parent.

My Asian Muslim identity in the Australian society was initially met with friendly curiosity. We were met with harmless double takes most of the time. Some brave people would break the ice with a smile and politely ask where we came from, or try to guess where I got my accent from. Within years of our migration this curiosity began to be overshadowed by suspicion and antagonism that came with changing global situations for Muslims.

Viewed from a macro level, this shift continues till today. Since the Gulf War in 1990 followed by the attack on 9/11 a decade later, lives of Muslims have never been the same again. No parenting books could have prepared us for this. Twenty years ago, the comments I received over our identity as Muslims were subtle but benign, such as, 'You have such beautiful girls. What a shame you have to cover them up!'

Then the backlash of terror attacks linked to Muslims cascaded down on Muslim communities like torrential rain especially for those living in the West. Misinformation about Islam, distortions, fear mongering and open attacks on Muslims worsened and continued to spread like wildfire. It was in such climate that my children and other Muslim children had to, and will continue to have to, negotiate for their space to exist. Parenting under these circumstances has not been a cruise to say the least.

On The Receiving End Of Islamophobia

My children and I have been verbally abused at supermarkets, at bus stops, or yelled at from cars that drove past on our walks in our neighbourhood, only because we were identifiable as Muslims. Here is our youngest daughter's experience. While she was completing her undergraduate studies she worked in a rug store. She had to mind the store on her own with access to her manager's support only by phone. Like most sales managers in retail she was alerted to watch out for theft.

She told me what she actually had to watch out for was more than the merchandise in the store. Her obvious 'Muslim-ness', identifiable through her wearing the hijab, meant that she had to look out for her own safety, especially when news reports of terror attacks were aired, regardless of where in the world these incidents took place. This awareness is very much a common reality for Muslims shrouded in the dark clouds of Islamophobia. My daughter had no way of knowing for sure what that something untoward would entail but she had to mentally prepare herself for anything between verbal abuse, physical assault, and possible vicious attacks.

Australia is relatively safe compared to some parts of the world where open discrimination against Muslims is trickled down from the attitude of their leaders. What could parenting experts possibly advise today's young Muslims to manage their wellbeing in this atmosphere if they themselves never knew what it was like to be the target of collective punishment from the society at large?

Living with this undercurrent of covert hostility as well as some people's overt prejudice and the possibility of physical assaults because of our faith is unnerving to most members of the Muslim community especially when some reports of Muslims being spat on, being abused and being attacked involve people we know. It is all too close for comfort.

Being on the alert and using one's common sense are essential. Having the tools and skills to regulate oneself is what I believe to be timely for the wellbeing of young Muslims. Support in this respect can come in many forms, but the most immediate are perspectives and practices they learn from their parents. The question is, to what extent do we as parents know how to regulate our own emotions and reactions in challenging situations?

It has been gradual but over the years I learned that not knowing what to do and getting off track is inevitable for a parenteer because we do not know our way. I learnt that the objective of parenting was never about staying perfectly on course all the time. Rather it is your *desire* to stay on track, and your *effort* to keep trying to get back on track that matters.

My task as a parent remains challenging, but I feel so much more positive about my role now because I learnt to stop aiming for results but instead to value the experience and learn from them.

Sometimes I question whether the positive changes

have taken place because I have grown older and hopefully wiser, or is it because my children have grown older and wiser? Would I have been receptive to what I know now back then? I do not know. Yet each and every one of my conversations with younger parents where I shared my insights have all been positively received.

What I Hope This Book Will Do For You

Parenting is a journey. I want this book to be a companion for those who care for children to care for themselves. Since parenteering is a journey for growth, I encourage you to keep a journal for your journey. Greater still, I encourage you to share your experiences, references and wisdom with me to enlighten other like-minded parents who consider taking care of their own wellbeing to last the distance.

This book takes its worldview from the Qur'an and Hadith—the teachings of Prophet Muhammad (peace and blessings be upon him). It is a worldview shared by not only Muslims who make up a fifth of the world's population,[4] but also other monotheist faith communities. I also use scholarly works in the field of parenting, education and positive psychology as references. I anticipate the perspectives I share will resonate with many of my readers, including values and principles I highlight in this book, regardless of their religious orientation.

Brief Outline Of This Book

Following the current introduction chapter, Chapter Two looks at Muslims' worldview and wellbeing goals, with an attempt at defining wellbeing from this perspective. The Positive Psychology movement headed by Martin Seligman around three decades ago injected much excitement and enthusiasm into the research of what makes people flourish. Seligman, hailed as the founder of Positive Psychology, turned the focus of psychological research from understanding and treating disorders to researching what makes the general population thrive. Chapter Two sets the scene for the Wellbeing Guide in this book.

Chapter Three introduces the first component of the Wellbeing Guide. It takes readers to look at the entire journey in terms of a 'One-Way Journey Home'. We may not know all there is to know about our journey, but we need to know where we are going and the nature of this journey. Life is a one-way journey. You may make U-turns along the way to change your course but you cannot take back the track you have passed. Once you embark on your journey, the timer starts ticking, you have only one direction to move forward, which is towards the exit. This exit point is the point that takes us home.

Chapter Four discusses the second component of the Wellbeing Guide. It offers a thinking and decision-making habit called: Two-Fold, Double-Selection process. Two-Fold reminds you to look beyond what is apparent to consider and discover the subtle behind the apparent. Look deeper than what meets the eye. Seek out its source and purpose. Double-Selection is a deliberate choice in decision-making. When you have a choice to make, you toss up between what your heart desires and what ultimately serves your wellbeing better; the latter may not always appeal to you at that point in time. Faith will guide you.

Practising this process gives you the guide to making better choices for your ultimate wellbeing.

Chapter Five offers an overview of the third component of the Wellbeing Guide: Three-Way Connection. Since the third component of the guide is further divided into three interconnected elements, this chapter invites readers to take an overview of the three elements. This chapter will be followed by Chapters Six to Eight, where a separate chapter is dedicated to each of the three elements to allow for in-depth understanding of this component.

Chapter Six explores Inward Connection. Inward Connection is concerned with a person's insight and relationship with the inner self. It includes a perspective of the makeup and natural tendencies of the self, understanding your own emotions and ways to improve how you manage them to make better choices in life. Knowledge of the self is the starting point for other connections. It is where your internal compass is housed. You are the driver for your journey.

Chapter Seven is on Vertical Connection. It refers to our spiritual connection with our Creator. From the self, we recognise the need to connect with someone other than the self—One who is greater, more powerful, eternal and immensely merciful. It concerns with the concepts that balance, still and nourish the soul; as well as practices to nurture the state of equilibrium within us. It enhances proper functioning of our internal compass.

Chapter Eight—External/Outward Connection—explains perspectives on our relationship with other creations and encounters in life, and how understanding of these concepts directs the way we interact with them.

When the inward and vertical connections are in place, outward connection becomes a means to attaining spiritual satisfaction as well as wellbeing in our earthly existence. The pathway and sequence of the Three-Way Connections may differ from one event to the next, but they are all interconnected and once these are practised on a regular basis, they loop back to the person's ultimate wellbeing—a state of peace and tranquillity of the heart.

Chapter Nine presents a number of scenarios where the Wellbeing Guide can be applied. Included in the chapter are a number of personal experiences where the Wellbeing Guide was put to action with satisfactory outcomes.

The final chapter discusses a virtue that every parent wants to have more of: that is, Sabr (patience). It reiterates the key messages of this book and encourages readers to implement the proposed Wellbeing Guide so they can enrich their own lives as a parenteer and let their positivity and calmness ripple onto their children.

CHAPTER TWO
Parenting For Ultimate Wellbeing—A Perspective

What is the life of this world but amusement and play? But verily the Home in the Hereafter–that is life indeed, if they but knew.[5]

CONTEMPORARY RESEARCHERS DISCUSS wellbeing in a range of dimensions, such as subjective, psychological, social, holistic perspectives, to name a few.

It is difficult to discuss wellbeing without taking into consideration one's life purpose. In *Reclaim Your Heart* Mogahed writes that there are two major worldviews concerning purpose in life. The first holds that this life on Earth is the Reality. This life is Everything. The second considers this life as a bridge in the context of God's Infinite Reality. All is fleeting in this life. One's life purpose in this view is to know, love and seek nearness to one's Creator.[6]

Consistent through all three Abrahamic religions is one message: to recognise and submit to the one and only God, for success in this life and in the Hereafter. From this standpoint, parenting for ultimate wellbeing is not only possible, it also makes the task of parenting less stressful, provided that one strives to live by the divine constitution for life, which is designed for humankind to live well.

To set the parameters of discussion for this book, I invite you to take a glance at a life that puts our spiritual existence at the fore. Seeing life through a holistic lens that includes our spirituality allows us to make sense of life matters and to live a life conducive to the health and wellbeing of our heart and mind. This is the basis of the ultimate wellbeing concept I wish to share with my readers.

This chapter is presented in two sections. The first section introduces a quick overview of one's life journey, inclusive of the life before and after this physical existence. The second section discusses wellbeing, how the concept of our worldview relates to wellbeing, and hence, how this connection is useful in nurturing one's own wellbeing first and foremost, and how it helps one to develop their children's wellbeing.

Section I: Life Journey—A Bird's Eye View

On a typical day a person may not think about big life questions such as where we came from and where we are heading. A free-spirited person may choose to wander the land without a set destination or a specific purpose. One has greater freedom to live how one likes when one is on his own. This changes when one becomes a parent. If you wear the hat of a parenteer, it becomes incumbent upon you to find out the answers to these questions. You are now responsible not only for yourself, but also for your children.

A simple analogy can be that of a teacher. Imagine you are taking a group of students on an excursion. It is essential that you know why, where and how you are going to take your students to a destination. This is the big picture. Even though you cannot foresee the whole journey, you as a parent needs to be mindful of the bigger picture.

For those whose worldview holds that this life is but a bridge, our lifespan consists of existence before and after the bridge. Many religions and philosophies hold that our life on Earth is only a part of the entire journey. Where were we before we came into our physical form? Where do we go after we leave this world? Different religions offer different perspectives on humans' spiritual existence.

From Islamic viewpoint, God in the Qur'an tells us that our existence began with our spiritual being before birth. At our appointed time we are born into this world clothed in our physical flesh. When our time to depart from this world arrives our body will decompose but our spiritual being will remain until the Final Day. After that the entire mankind will be resurrected for the Final Judgment. Mankind will be judged, and then sent to their Final Abode—Paradise or Hell. This worldview is the basis of how Muslims perceive their purpose in life.

The Spiritual Existence

We cannot talk about our existence without acknowledging our spiritual being (or 'rooh' in Arabic). This spiritual being needs and seeks to connect with its Creator. Man has a tendency to neglect this need and often feels self-sufficient or too arrogant to make a connection with God. However, when people find themselves in a life and death situation, many automatically raise their hands or look up to the sky to ask for help. Whether we acknowledge it or not, there is a connection between us and God.

In addition, there has to be more to our physical form when we consider our conscience, our higher order thinking abilities, ability to empathise, to feel, etc. What is it in addition to our physical being that is experiencing these?

I accept the explanation that we are innately linked to our Creator.

I believe once we accept humans' spiritual existence and connection to our Creator, our purpose in life starts to take on a whole new perspective, and therefore, new meaning. In the Qur'an, human race began with the creation of the first human, Adam (peace be upon him).[7]

From him, God created his spouse, Hawa (Eve) and from them both, God created their offspring, and thus began the human race.[8]

Our spiritual connection and higher faculties to process knowledge and make choices are what make us the noblest creation of God. A verse in the Qur'an, 'When I have fashioned him and breathed My spirit [rooh] into him…' tells us that this rooh in us is the element of life, a gift of God that was created to make us uniquely human.[9]

The word in Arabic in the text is sometimes translated as spirit, while other translations use the word soul. To avoid getting this word confused by its translations, I wish to use the Arabic word rooh throughout this book. Another Arabic word I will use in its Arabic form is nafs.

According to Abu Bilal Mustafa Al-Kanadi, the

majority of scholars consider rooh and nafs one and the same and both terms can be used interchangeably.[10]

A distinction some have made is that rooh is the element of life throughout the journey of human species, i.e. before and after the earthly existence, and when we are returned to our final abode. Sajid Umar explains that when this element of life (rooh) is joined with the physical body outside the mother's womb, it is called nafs.[11]

Some use the terms personality, self, or ego to represent the word nafs. A section will be dedicated to more detailed discussion of human nafs in Chapters Five and Six. Understanding what nafs is about and how we can manage our nafs is of great importance in personal development because nafs is the form we can exercise control over while we exist in our worldly life.

Concerning the rooh, very little is revealed to Prophet Muhammad (peace and blessings be upon him). Of the little that is made known to us is the rooh's existence and its knowledge of our Creator. God informs us in the Qur'an that all creatures, including humankind, acknowledged His Lordship and submitted to His Sovereignty when we were created.

Muslims acknowledge a human's dependent nature and our need to worship this higher being. We are encouraged to call upon God for any need, who is All Powerful, Omnipresent and Everlasting.

Coming Into Physical Being

It was not until recently through knowledge of human anatomy and advancement in medical science that we came to know the sequence and description of foetal development. Not many people are aware that this embryological development was revealed to us in its precise order in the Qur'an on numerous occasions more than fourteen centuries ago.[12]

Prophet Muhammad (peace and blessings be upon him) also informed us that at around 120 days of conception, the person's rooh is being blown into the foetus.[13]

God is capable of all things. Just like how Prophet Jesus (peace be upon him) was conceived, people of faith understand that when God decrees an affair, He only says to it: 'Be! And it is!'[14]

The human foetus has a spiritual being and continues to develop physically for several months until it reaches its viable form ready to be born into this world.

We have no recollection of our full submission to God before we came to this Earth. As we grow, we gradually become aware of our surroundings and of ourselves in this physical world.

Like it or not, human bodies continue to submit to God's system. Every moment we live, we are in submission to God at our cellular level, such as our digestive and cardiovascular systems, except what our free will can command, such as movement and thinking. This freedom is a privilege, but also a test. All God asks from us is to choose to submit our whole being to acknowledge Him. If we ignored this duty, we have wasted this opportunity. There will be no other chance to submit to God after this worldly life. Everyone wishes on their deathbed that they made most of that window of opportunity to serve God.

Life After Death

An inquisitive mind would want to ask—what happens after one dies? This is where belief in life in the Hereafter and a Final Judgment will help answer these puzzling questions. The Qur'an tells us that there are actually three phases of life after we die. The first phase is life in the grave until the Last Day when finally everything dies except the Creator who is ever-living. After that the entirety of humankind will be resurrected to face judgment, and lastly we will be sent to our final abode to live in eternity.

We learn that the body dies but the essence of human, the rooh, continues its journey. In a way, we can liken this physical body to a suit that we wear for our appointed time in this world. Just like we put on our scuba diving gear when we go into the ocean (this physical world), we take off our costume when we leave the ocean while the essence of our being continues to journey.

The human life is much more than this fleshy casing.

It was reported in the UK in 2017 that a ground-breaking research has 'confirmed' that there was life for up to three minutes after a person's heart had stopped functioning. Almost 40% of the 2060 patients who had near death experiences from cardiac arrests recalled some form of awareness after they had been pronounced dead. Scientists have discovered that consciousness continues even after the heart stops.[15]

This remains a contentious issue to sceptics until further proof becomes available.

As Muslims we have no trouble believing that there is some awareness of the deceased in the grave. Prophet Muhammad (peace and blessings be upon him) said that the deceased can hear the footsteps of his friends and relatives leaving the grave, and that will be the time when he is questioned about his faith. We have increasingly taken as fact information we have gained in recent times that our minds could not have imagined nor accepted before. Know that we have not uncovered *all* truths, if humankind ever will. In time we may reach a point where life after death will become a fact; for now, it is a test of faith for those who believe.

The Concept Of Life After Death

To help one grasp the concept of life after death, let us take a look at our state of being in our sleep. We all know that when we fall asleep we lose awareness of what is happening around us. We cannot recall when we turn from side to side. However, in our dreams we feel emotions, such as fear, sadness, frustration, anger, happiness, joy, excitement and so on; we go to places and talk to people. We recognise our loved ones and interact with people we may or may not know. We even think and process information in our dreams, all the while without much movement of our body, or exercising our free will like we do when we are awake.

According to Islamic teachings, sleep is called small death. In the Qur'an we are told, 'It is He who calls your souls back by night, knowing what you have done by day, then raises you up again in the daytime until your fixed term is fulfilled.'[16]

Sometimes we remember what/whom we saw or where we went in our dreams. Other times we wake up feeling we had dreams yet having no clear memory of them at all.

For those whose souls are not returned to their bodies during their sleep, that is when their time on Earth has come to an end. Muslims reaffirm this belief by making supplications daily. I have chosen the shortest of the many supplications our Prophet (peace and blessings be upon him) taught us to say as a demonstration—we say, 'In Your name O Allah, I die and I live' before going to sleep. We prepare to depart from this world every night. Being able to wake up in the morning means that we have been given another day to serve God on Earth. We take our new lease in life to be our best self, every day, for as long as we live. As soon as we wake up we say, 'All praises be to the One who gives us life after our death and to Him will be our final return.'

Why Believe In Life After Death?

People who are cynical about what happens after death are unable to say what next. I would advise them to at least consider the possibility that there is life after death. Believing in life in the Hereafter may just help one find answers and most importantly, the peace to many mind-boggling questions one may have about life.

For instance, human limitations have resulted in errors in judgment whereby an innocent person is sentenced to decades of imprisonment for a crime he never committed. Here is my question: how does anyone repay this person for the freedom and prime years robbed from him? Unless one believes there is a higher being who promises of a court that will recompense every person in absolute fairness, how does one reconcile with such injustice? In the Qur'an our Creator promises us His absolute justice. Is there any other avenue for the innocent victims to endure injustice or atrocities committed against them except with faith and hope for a day when ultimate justice will be served?

Then there are those who strive to do the right thing, like those who have studied hard for an examination, hoping for a day when their perseverance, patience, sacrifice and good work will be rewarded. In fact those who choose to follow the divine guidance are doing themselves a great favour to find peace.

Said Nursi, a twentieth century Kurdish theologian, writes this about the Hereafter:

> Does it make sense that we should remain unrecompensed and unanswerable, that the Majestic One of Splendor and Glory should not prepare a realm of requital for us?[17] [...]We cannot flee or hide in nothingness or enter the ground, just as we cannot conceal ourselves from the All-Powerful and Majestic One to Whose Power all future contingencies and all past events bear witness, and Who creates winter and spring which, taken together, resemble the Resurrection. Since we are not properly called to account and judged while in this world, we must proceed to a Supreme Tribunal and lasting happiness in another.[18]

Parents who use this worldview as their road map to guide their children will likely raise children who will choose to do good for goodness' sake and who are better equipped to deal with tough and sometimes incomprehensible trials in life.

Resurrection

Many people wonder how can we be brought to life again after our bodies have crumbled into dust?

More than fourteen centuries ago Prophet Muhammad (peace and blessings be upon him) informed us how humankind will be resurrected. He said that 'there is nothing of the human body that does not decay except one bone; that is the little bone at the end of the coccyx of which the human body will be recreated on the Day of Resurrection'.[19]

For those who wish to hear what science has to say about this, the following scientific evidence may be of help.

In 1935, Hans Spemann won the Nobel Prize for his discovery of the Primary Organiser. Over several years of experimenting, Spemann and his colleague found the crushed and boiled coccyx bone still having the ability to grow in a secondary embryo.[20]

In other words, they found the coccyx bone to be indestructible.

One may ask, how about those who choose to have their bodies cremated after death? In 1994 Dr Othman Aljilani and Sheikh Abd Al Majid Azzindani carried out experiments on burning the coccyx bones on stones and burnt them until their total combustion where the bones turned from red to black. The carbonised pieces were sent for analysis by Dr Al-Olaki, a professor in histology and pathology at Sanaa University. He found that the cells of the bone tissues of the coccyx survived the burning and were not affected. Dr. Aljilani concluded that the above experiment showed the survival of the primary organiser even after burning, was proof that the Prophet's statement that 'the coccyx bone does not decay' was true.[21]

We believe the Day of Resurrection is a major event along the journey of our rooh that will take place. That will be the day when the entire humankind will be raised from our tiny coccyx bones into our full form like a seed that develops into a plant, ready to be judged, then rewarded or sentenced for what we did in our life on Earth.

Final Judgment And Destination

The day when we are raised from death will be the day when all humankind from the beginning till the end of time are gathered in an assembly. That is when ultimate justice will be served.

At the end of the full account, everyone will be sent to their eternal abode—either home to paradise or hell. Those who strove to obey their Lord and did good deeds in their worldly life will be granted paradise out of His Mercy, and those who transgressed and spread mischief on Earth will be given hell as their final abode.

Knowledge of our existence, physically and spiritually, is critical to our wellbeing. Our physical existence is the only period we can exercise our free will to work towards our final destination. We are given multiple opportunities after our small death each day to make sound choices in this world as an investment for the Hereafter.

My attempt at summing up this journey into a simplified diagram for readers who are visual learners like myself is found in Figure 1, listing references where appropriate.

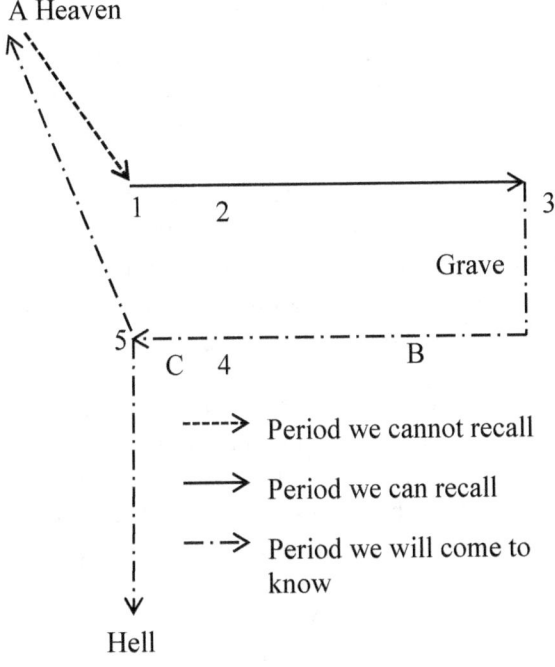

1 Conception
2 Birth
3 Death
4 Resurrection
5 Day of Judgment
A When humans testified God's Lordship (Qur'an 7:172)
B Life in the grave (Al-Bukhari 2.461)
C Between Resurrection and Judgment (Qur'an 75:1-11)

Figure 1: Islamic Perspective of the Journey of the Human Soul

Section II: Wellbeing

So far I hope I have convinced my fellow *parenteers*, not necessarily to agree with what I shared, but to see the importance in seeking answers to the big questions in life. You, as captain of the crew, may not have travelled this route before, but your crew is counting on you to know where you are taking them. If we bear in mind that we are both physical and spiritual beings, we cast our sight beyond the horizon with our innate knowing—more than just the here and now. We realise the urgency in seeking out what gives us wellbeing in this life and life in the Hereafter and we strive to live our life to achieve both objectives simultaneously. It is similar to choosing the food we eat. For the here and now, we eat to satiate our hunger. If this was the only objective, then we eat what we can get our hands on as quickly as we can. If we are also concerned about our health and wellbeing in the long run, we would make different choices to satisfy both our hunger and sustained health. This is the ultimate wellbeing I am encouraging parents to aim for.

In this section we take a look at a few theories on wellbeing, then I will tender my definition of wellbeing and how this definition informs parenting.

Perspectives On Wellbeing

The word wellbeing is synonymous with wellness. Its meaning extends beyond the traditional concept for health or happiness. Efforts to understand and research aspects of wellbeing have contributed to an ever-expanding body of knowledge, especially in the recent two to three decades.

To date there is no consensus on the definition of wellbeing. A literature review conducted by Dodge, Daly, Huyton and Sanders reports that definitions of wellbeing have mostly been presented in its descriptive elements.[22] This is demonstrated in the various theories on identifying what contributes to wellbeing, rather than defining it. For example, Seligman's Wellbeing Theory considers wellbeing as a construct. This theory proposes five elements that contribute to wellbeing: Positive Emotion, Engagement, Relationships, Meaning and Purpose, and Accomplishment (PERMA).[23] Similarly, the National Wellness Institute in the USA looks at six dimensions of wellness: physical, social, intellectual, spiritual, emotional and occupational wellness.[24]

Wellbeing Versus Happiness

Wellbeing is sometimes linked to success and quality of life.

Are successful people happy?

The traditional formula of working hard to achieve success and that success makes you happy is outdated. Harvard researcher Shawn Achor proposes that this formula ought to be worked backwards.[25] By this he means that successful people are not necessarily happy but happy people are more likely to become successful. In other words, happiness increases our capacity to learn, contributes to wellbeing, and in turn, wellbeing facilitates success.

Happiness can be subjective. Certain pleasures are fleeting, such as the adrenalin rush one gets when playing a video game. Therefore subjective happiness alone is not a reliable indicator to a person's overall wellbeing status.

Likewise, certain not-so-pleasant activities may prove to be important contributors to one's long term wellbeing. An example of this is working out instead of spending hours on gaming.

Other aspects of human existence, such as spiritual connection, altruism, meaning and purpose, living by values and morals have also been associated with positively contributing to a person's wellbeing.

Parents play an important role in guiding and establishing habits that are likely to benefit their children in the long run. I feel a sense of duty at this point to bring my readers onto the same page with me about the parameters of the very broad subject of wellbeing.

Firstly, let us consider ultimate wellbeing.

As we cast our sight from the physical and transient to include our spiritual wellbeing and what goes beyond our earthly existence, our take on 'success' defined by society shifts.

Secondly, wellbeing can be developed.

The most encouraging message I take away from Achor's work is that happiness is not a birth privilege. Everyone can work to achieve higher levels of happiness, irrespective of their gender, social status, or their individual endowment such as intelligence or wealth.

Achor proposes that wellbeing can be learned and developed. It is the kind of wellbeing that even when you are in physical pain, suffering emotionally, or being dealt unfairly, you have the mindset and purpose that pulls you back from the brink of despair, and you have the tools and determination to endure the hardship in order to bounce back.

Wellbeing Defined

My proposed state of wellbeing can be likened to the state of preparedness and calmness experienced by a committed student. Her day-to-day existence is made up of a string of choices that paves her way towards her final examination with quiet confidence. Although she does not have complete control over the outcome of her examination, she can walk out from it knowing that she has done her best to prepare for it. This knowing gives her a sense of peace. This is an oversimplified analogy to help us get a glimpse of what the state of 'the self at peace' (nafs al-mutmainnah) may be like.

Here I propose my definition of wellbeing rather differently from what is currently available in the literature that I have come across this far. I define wellbeing as **a state of serenity,**[26] **attained through one's conscious alignment**[27] **of the fluctuating heart**[28] **with divine guidance.**

My view on the objective of wellbeing comes from the Qur'an, 'The day when wealth and children will not benefit anyone except he who will come to God with a sound heart (Qalb-e-Saleem).'[29]

How can one attain a sound heart? Simply, one who believes and engages in aligning his life in remembrance and obedience to God will have cultivated a sound heart that is in a state of 'self at peace' (nafs al mutmainnah).[30] This remembrance is not referring to someone retreating from the society and devoting his entire life to prayers as a recluse. Rather it is about the extent of one's mindfulness of his Creator. It is about a purposeful alignment of every intention and every action we take in life with what is pleasing to our Creator.

To achieve this, we must strive to invest our life now for a destination of eternal peace and satisfaction. The present physical life is the only opportunity we get to exercise our freedom of choice to actively work towards the goal of attaining a tranquil heart. This is in sync with Emily Dickinson, who is quoted to have said, 'Forever—is composed of Nows.'[31]

Keep in mind it is in our nature that we will go off course, make mistakes or make wrong choices along the way. Being mindful of our Creator helps us recognise the need to spring clean and purge unwanted clutter within ourselves, to amend our wrongdoings and to improve our behaviour, in preparation to arrive at our destination with a sound heart. We strive to achieve this state of wellbeing by journeying through this world with the end in mind.

PARENTING FOR ULTIMATE WELLBEING

We will be judged individually by our intent and actions with respect to the resources and trials God has given us. Those who are incapable of making this conscious choice due to mental incapacities are free from blame. Those who desire but are unable to materialise their choice due to various reasons are judged not by the outcome, but by their intention and effort.[32]

Do not think for a moment that one who chooses success in the Hereafter is morbid and dull. Striving for ultimate serenity is a two-fold investment. You benefit from contentment and a clear conscience in both worlds.

Watering the Roots

The Wellbeing Guide in this book aims to help parents work towards this state of 'the self at peace'. It is a state of tranquillity and contentment that connects to the spiritual, physical, psychological, intellectual, emotional and social dimensions of wellbeing. The process involves an ongoing development and evolvement of the self. It is a lifelong pursuit. It goes beyond the realms of hedonistic pleasures and successes in worldly affairs. It is about harnessing and aligning the free will to submit to divine guidance for success in this world and the eternal life in the Hereafter.

This perspective of wellbeing and the aligning of your choices and actions with divine guidance pave the way to developing a sound heart. The alignment process involves regular mindful practices and reflections of the proposed 1-2-3 Wellbeing Guide to be elaborated in the subsequent chapters of this book. This guide, when practised, helps to recognise and silence the chatter, stills the heart, and tames the desires. It keeps the mind and limbs active and productive in times of ease, and provides buoyancy and hope in times of turbulence.

In an age rife with uncertainties and alarming statistics of mental illnesses among young people, parents' influence and support for their children cannot be overemphasised. The seas are not getting any calmer for Muslims in the foreseeable future. Although this Wellbeing Guide by its title is proposed to parents, the real impact I am counting on is its rippling effects on the younger generation. This guide combines basic wellbeing principles and Muslims' core values into an easy to remember guide to help parents with their monumental task—to raise the next generation who are wholesome, balanced, compassionate, confident and grounded human beings.

This book validates your struggles and invites you to look at wellbeing perspectives you might not have thought of before. It allows you to look at yourself with new lenses and offers you ways to connect your core values to your role as parents. It is hoped that through your regular practice and modelling, you impart your vision and skills to prepare your children to weather the possible storms ahead with a deep sense of purpose and serenity.

CHAPTER THREE
Wellbeing Guide First Component: One-Way Journey Home

From the very moment of creation, mankind is on a journey and he is not allowed to halt except when he reaches Paradise or Hellfire.[33]

HOW DOES THE Muslim worldview benefit someone's wellbeing? Researchers of wellbeing and positive psychology have conducted in-depth studies on what makes one's life meaningful.[34] It makes every sense to live our life with a purpose. We want to exit from this world having tried to fulfill that purpose. Of course it helps to know what that purpose is. I propose the concept 'One-Way Journey Home' as a starting point. It is shared by all Abrahamic faith groups. It puts life and death on centre stage. It motivates you to find the wall against which you lean your ladder for your journey in life.

What Does One-Way Journey Home Mean?

As exhibited in the diagram in the previous chapter (Figure 1, Chapter Two), this simplified illustration of a Muslim's worldview provides us with a bird's eye view of the entire journey. It is intended to clarify where we came from and where we are heading towards. In Stephen Covey's *Seven Habits of Highly Effective People*, his second habit is 'begin with the end in mind'. [35] This is a call for those who wish to live an effective and balanced life to work backwards. In other words, it is getting us to imagine what kind of a life we wish to live by picturing how we want to be remembered after we die. However, our end in this book is somewhat different to Covey's end. Covey's end stops at the exit point of the physical life. The focus Covey asks people to think about is how we impact on those who are living, including generations to come, and what legacies one leaves behind that are of benefit to humanity. For altruistic people, Covey's 'begin with the end in mind' habit is highly motivating. It does not answer the question for those who asks, 'What's in it for me?'

When we look at life purpose as an opportunity to invest in our own wellbeing through submitting and worshipping our Lord, the paradigm shifts. No one is left out. Anyone who wishes to attain success and ultimate wellbeing is covered.

As explained in the previous chapter, people from majority of faith communities believe in life after death. Religion or no religion, no one disputes that there is a definite end time for each of us, and that we are all moving towards our individually timed end point. To those who believe in life in the Hereafter, death is the end point of our physical existence in this temporary world, and at the same time the beginning of the next leg of our journey that takes us home. It is a similar concept between the terms 'graduation' and 'commencement'. Graduation is referring to one having completed a stage of studies whereas commencement means that as well as entering a new phase in life.

Our concern is what kind of home we want for ourselves. Someone who desires to one day build his own home needs to have a clear idea what that home will be like. Where do you want to build it and why? How big do you want your home to be and for what purpose? How much money do you have to save up towards this dream home? This is what I mean by backward planning. You start by having your dream home in mind then work backwards to outline your milestones. From each milestone you break down detailed steps so that your lifestyle is geared towards fulfilling your goal.

Your 'One-Way Journey Home' takes you to your final abode in the Hereafter. This journey entails how we spend our time, what we engage in, what we wish to bring with us, who we want to meet after the Final Judgment. As simple as it sounds, that is our *purpose.*

We need to live for our purpose now. Imagine the time in transit in an airport is the only chance you get to arrange your food, lodging, transport and occupation before your next flight arrived, would you snooze away your time or sit idly playing on your electronic gadgets? Or would you make the most of the internet and time to the best of your ability to plan for the rest of your journey?

I urge parents to bear this analogy in mind to teach our children early on that each of us is in transit on Earth to prepare for our journey home. The chance to make effort to build our eternal home is now, i.e. the time we have on this Earth. No one knows how long one has. The average person may be given six or seven decades, some may be given more, while others are given much less.

If we believe in life in the Hereafter, we have a definite purpose. Imagine waking up every day saving up for, designing and working towards your everlasting home. Each day is a gift from God to live our best moment. Each step we take paves our way to our everlasting home. What that everlasting home will be like is up to you to work for. The choice is yours.

Introduce One-Way Journey Home To Children

To help your child grasp this concept, take them for a tour to a store where there is only one way to get to the exit. The first time I visited a store designed with such concept many years ago caught my attention. I did not have much time when I entered that store. There was only one way to the exit. The store was strategically set up to make customers walk pass all the items from beginning till the end in one direction only. The 'short-cuts' may allow you to skip one or two display sections but you still have to go through most of the maze to get to the exit. I do not intend to discuss the marketing psychology behind this design. What I wish to bring to your attention is to see it as a concrete example to help your child understand the 'One-Way Journey Home' concept of our life. The following scenarios may help with your discussion.

Scenario 1

In this scenario, you were merely window-shopping. You went in but did not have anything in mind to buy, like what I did the first time I set foot in that store.

You passed through the displays without a clear purpose. At the exit point, you walked out with nothing except some idea of what was available in the store. If you wanted something later, your knowledge of what was available would help. You could always go back to it.

Scenario 2

You entered the store knowing what you were looking for. You had specific items you wanted and you were also mindful of the closing time.

In this scenario, you entered the store with a purpose because you checked the most recently published catalogue beforehand and you were clear of what you wanted from the store. The quickest possible way to get what you need and make it to the check out before closing is to find a map of the store to help you get to where you want to go, pick up what you need then you won't have to fret when the store closes.

Scenario 3

You consider it your right to do what you like in the store. Admittedly this scenario is a little ridiculous but nonetheless worth discussing.

Let me share with you what I once witnessed. I have done a fair bit of travelling. On one of my overseas trips

I went to a one-way-to-the-exit store two hours before its closing time. Like all franchise stores, its set up was almost identical to all other such stores I visited in other countries. However, the customers I witnessed in this store were extraordinary. Most of the adults seemed oblivious to how their children behaved in there. The messiest area was in the children's bedroom section. Sheets on the display beds were messy and some had small shoe marks. I saw children grabbing soft toys out of big tubs, dragging them along then throwing them on the floor when their eyes caught sight of something else. I must say that was one of the most thought-provoking shopping trips I had ever experienced.

As I stood in the long queue at the checkout, I imagined the extra time all the shop attendants would have to spend, restoring the displays back to their designated spots, changing the sheets, making up the beds and sofas, and picking up what looked like hundreds of soft toys strewn all over the shop.

Granted, what I witnessed that evening was when it was nearing the store's closing time on a weekend. To be fair not all children behaved in the same manner. It might have been a particularly busy day for argument's sake.

Call me a drama queen if you want. The mess I saw told me it could not have been the work of just a handful of children! What I witnessed that evening got me thinking: what will become of these youngsters? In life every action has its consequence. We either see it immediately or later down the track. Just because a consequence is not immediate doesn't mean there is none.

This is my point about the last scenario. We were not created to live alone. Everyone has his/her rights. We were never meant to live our life to do whatever we desired without consequences. We will be held to account at some point. This is where believing in the final judgment in the Hereafter makes sense.

The Store Scenarios And Early Adolescents

You can use the one-way exit store analogy to discuss many concepts with your children.

First Scenario

The first scenario introduces the concept of valuing life with each day we are blessed. It motivates us to make most out of what we have now. If one values one's life's purpose, we would not want to stroll through this life as a window-shopper, or doing a trial run hoping to return in another life and live it for real the second time. Life does not offer you a rehearsal or a preview. We are on our 'One-Way Journey Home' right now. Like it or not, we are all moving towards our timed exits. Be grateful for each day we are given, for each day is a brand-new opportunity. Although we cannot undo what is done, or to relive yesterday, last week, or last year, we can strive to do better as each new day comes.

Make the many NOWs count. We may not be able to undo what we missed yesterday, but we can definitely decide to do better with every new NOW we are given, as long as we live with a clear purpose.

Second Scenario

The second scenario emphasises the importance of finding a map in life and using our inbuilt compass to live our life to the fullest. Here I wish to underscore the importance of referring to an updated catalogue. How absolutely thoughtful are store managements to go to the trouble to inform potential customers of their latest products, what are still available, how much they cost and how they can benefit our lives?

Do you not wish that there were an updated directory to guide us in life? The fact is, the most updated and final version of life manual from our Creator *is* right here in our hands. It is the Qur'an. It is the final revelation given to the last and final prophet in the chain of prophets God has sent to mankind. Prophet Muhammad (peace and blessings be upon him) came to confirm all divine revelations before us—the scroll of Abraham, the Torah of Moses, the Psalms of David and the Bible of Jesus (peace be upon them all). Using the analogy of different editions of the same book, the Qur'an is the most updated scripture from God. Together with the Hadith of our beloved Prophet Muhammad (peace and blessings be upon him) they are the map and manual that guide us to our final destination. It is complete with dos and don'ts and examples of nations in the past, of how they lived and the consequences of their actions and more. It illustrates for us the kind of 'homes' we can choose to work on attaining. It lists all there is to do for our final abode.

Third Scenario

The last scenario can be related to obeying rules and making responsible choices. Freedom and responsibility are good topics for discussion with early adolescents.

Ask your child what they think freedom is and why is it a privilege to be given freedom to choose? Discuss with them how can freedom be sustained. What will happen if everyone does as they wish without a concern over the impact of their actions on others? The consequences will always find their way back to you; if not now, definitely later. Urge your young adolescents to think about how they want to travel through this journey. Would they follow guidelines and behave accordingly?

Explain to them that people who save up to build their own house must have discipline in order to live on a budget. Their expenses are carefully thought out and spent for specific purposes.

Benefits Of The One-Way Journey Home Concept

Benefits of the 'One-Way Journey Home' are many. As human beings, we have been endowed with the unique gift of choosing at free will, to some extent. We do not have control over all things, such as who our parents are, what our skin colour is, how long we live, how well our faculties or internal organs function etc. We are not held accountable for these matters, because these are not matters that involve our choice. Where we are held accountable is when things are within our control. It is by our intention and our efforts that we will be judged, not the outcome. We must acknowledge and appreciate the ability we have been given to make conscious choices within what is humanly possible, and use it to our benefit before we get to our individually timed end point in life.

I wish to highlight two significant benefits of putting this concept into practice for wellbeing: purposeful existence and delayed gratification.

Purposeful Existence

Learning from our shopping scenarios in the previous section, you may want to be selective in what you pack into your trolleys to take to the check out within the time frame you have been given. You may not have thought about this before, but as each day comes you are packing your deeds to go home. Each day is a new chance for us to sort through what we wish to change, discard or keep, as well as what new items we wish to add to our suitcases. Parents who live by the concept of 'One-Way Journey Home' live a purposeful existence with their children. They spend their time on productive activities. They strive to do the right thing by God. They try to be mindful of their intention, of what they do and say. They reflect and desire to do better.

Younger children emulate adults in their lives. They learn through observation and play. They may not be able to understand the concept of time management yet. Games that use a timer can help children become aware of the value of time. The five daily calls to prayer punctuate the day into smaller sections. Older children develop their values through questions and debates. Discussing the 'One-Way Journey Home' concept with your adolescent and older children help them develop mindfulness of the bigger picture: their purpose in life. They learn to appreciate rules instead of rebelling against them. This is the concept behind the practice of aligning our needs and our minds with our hearts using the Qur'an and teachings of our prophet as our map and manual.

Delayed Gratification

The famous Stanford 'marshmallow' experiments led by Professor Walter Mischel since the late 1960s tested pre-schoolers' ability to delay gratification. In their initial tests a group of children aged around four years were given the option of eating a small treat or wait for up to fifteen minutes alone for a bigger and more preferred treat.[36] Follow up studies of some of the original participants after they turned fifteen and subsequent tests found correlations between the children's ability to delay gratification and academic achievements and fewer behaviour problems. Those who demonstrated ability to delay gratification when they were four years old were found to have 'developed into more cognitively and socially competent adolescents, achieving higher scholastic performance and coping better with frustration and stress.'[37]

Criticisms of the 'marshmallow test' argue that ability to delay gratification was not a reliable factor to predict success later in life. Other factors such as family background, poverty and intelligence have also been found to correlate to success.[38] In defence of the original studies, I understand it was never intended to make delayed gratification as the magic prescription for success later in life. Delaying gratification remains a useful life skill and positive character trait for exercising self-regulation and discipline towards attaining long-term goals.

To me, a Muslim's life is just like a series of marshmallow tests, with many small and big marshmallow tests bobbing up along the way to test us. Believers are informed about what is good for them in the long run over what is pleasing to their lower desires; just like how the four-year-olds were given the choice between eating the small treat and waiting for the bigger treat in Mischel's marshmallow test. The good can sometimes be accompanied by difficulties and hard work. It requires a person to want the bigger reward enough to stay patient during the waiting period. Understanding our personal strengths and weaknesses and learning how to manage the struggles of our inner self is half the battle won. More details on our inner self is discussed in Inward Connection in Chapter Five.

Being mindful of our 'One-Way Journey Home' is a reminder to control our desires. Patience without purpose is suffering. In this temporary life there are full of things tangible and intangible that appeal to our lower desires for immediate gratification. We are constantly tempted to indulge in such immediate pleasures, many of which when consumed in excess, lead to destructive consequences to the self and sometimes to others as well. To resist succumbing to our lower desires, we need to strengthen our muscles of patience and endurance for a higher purpose.

We can train ourselves to delay gratifying our immediate pleasure for that which builds our eternal wellbeing. Like saving up to buy quality construction material and items for the new home we are building, we make sacrifices and discipline ourselves to budget and use our resources wisely. With the vision of a new permanent home in sight, we treat the house we currently live with a totally different mind frame. This concept reminds us of the 'bigger picture', it puts the nitty-gritties of our everyday life into perspective. It sets the direction of our focus right from the beginning of our journey. Frequent reference to this concept gives us meaning in what we choose to do and helps to align our actions with our goals in life amidst all forms of temptations and trials of this temporary life.

Conclusion

Viewing our life as a journey towards our everlasting home in the Hereafter is a reminder to live our purpose and to restrain our lower desires. We work on our submission and obedience to God for our ultimate wellbeing. It helps us appreciate why we do what we do and why we abstain from what we try to keep away from, even if it means we are seen as strangers. We aim to return to our *permanent home* with a sound heart because after departing from this world we will continue on our journey paved by our choices and actions we invested while we were alive on Earth.

Ibn Qayyim wrote about choosing between two pleasures and two hardships.[39] These are the temporary and eternal pleasures, and the temporary and eternal hardships. One must know that it is better for eternal pleasures to follow temporary hardship than it is for eternal hardship to follow temporary pleasure. This brings us to the second component of the Wellbeing Guide: 'Two-Fold, Double-Selection', in Chapter Four.

CHAPTER FOUR

Wellbeing Guide Second Component: Two-Fold, Double-Selection

The same wind that uproots trees makes the grasses shine. The lordly wind loves the weakness and lowness of grasses. Never brag of being strong.[40]

THIS CHAPTER INTRODUCES the second component of the Wellbeing Guide. It has two sections: Two-Fold and Double-Selection. Two-Fold is a concept that serves as a reminder to think deeper than what is in front of us in day-to-day encounters and also as an emergency brake when we are under pressure. Most assuredly, this concept when applied avails a person of a chance to dive deeper into a situation. It often helps one to recognise the finer details of an object to gain new appreciation for an encounter. Double-Selection is a concept to guide a person in choice-making. When raising children, parents will definitely be tested. Implementation of this component prevents parents from overreacting, and allows them to make choices that are better for all in the long run. When practised regularly, Two-Fold and Double-Selection can improve our wellbeing and increase in our wisdom.

Two-Fold

Some time ago, motivated by my own wellbeing guidelines, I set out to learn the Beautiful Names and Attributes of God. The most salient point for me in that course was learning the apparent meaning as well as the subtle, the general as well as the specific attributes of God. This was where I got my inspiration for the first part of the second component of my proposed Wellbeing Guide: Two-Fold.

The first fold is what is apparent. Everything has its outward appearance, shape, colour, characteristics and so forth. Every object and every encounter/event has its façade, or what is immediately presented to us. Whatever enters into our perception is the first fold.

When we encounter the first fold, we can take it as a prompt for us to explore the messages behind each object and each encounter, we allow ourselves the chance to explore the second fold.

The Two-Fold concept encourages us to look further and deeper than what is being manifested.

First Fold—In Day-To-Day Encounters

The Two-Fold concept allows us the opportunity to acknowledge there is always more to what is apparent.

Watering the Roots

There is always more to discover, to learn; in other words, we look deeper into what we see. I believe many of us often practise 'Two-Fold' without realising. Babies see things literally. As they get older, their caregivers start to play peek-a-boo with them. They learn to look behind what is in front of their eyes hoping to find the adult's face. They learn to connect the caregiver's voice they hear to his/her presence even if the latter is out of sight in the next room. As our knowledge and experience expand, we become more skilled at making inferences and meaning out of what we encounter.

For example, we come across corn being sold at the market. Our first fold information gathering may include the selling price and how fresh it is. Our second fold is done later, if we allow ourselves to think deeper.

As adults, we rarely come across anything without any thoughts occurring. Investigators and detectives are trained to uncover hidden clues that the untrained eye can easily miss. Thinking Two-Fold is a way for us to establish a habit of pondering upon what is behind what we see. This helps us to derive meaning, and to better appreciate what is presented.

The second fold is beholder-dependent. In the case of the corn one's thoughts may go to the farmers. If the price is higher than average, one may want to know what bumped up the price. If the price is exceptionally low, we may wonder if there are any visible flaws to the crop; or if there were other factors that caused the price to drop. I do not know about you, my heart always goes out to the farmers when a produce is sold at a much lower price than the norm.

Two-Fold As An Emergency Brake

Pondering over what is behind an encounter is a luxury when one is under pressure. How does the Two-Fold concept apply when split second decisions need to be made on the spot, or when our emotions are stirred up so high that we often speak or act without thinking?

Under these circumstances, the Two-Fold concept acts as an emergency brake. When we do not have time or the headspace to dwell on what is behind our encounter, merely thinking of Two-Fold may be just what it takes to step on the brake and prevent us from acting on impulse.

Challenges, hardship, trials and unexpected experiences are part and parcel of life. When things do not go as planned, or when the stakes are high, or when one is under the constraints of time, or being pressured to survive on overstretched resources, humans naturally switch into a fight or flight mode. The underlying emotions can be one of frustration, embarrassment, hurt, anger, fear, humiliation, despair etc., or a combination of any of these emotions.

Let us face it, very few of us are able to control our reactive behaviour when we are put under pressure. As much as I hate to admit, there have been several occasions when I succumbed to fear of missing out on seemingly 'once-in-a-lifetime' bargains in a small window of opportunity designed to entice gullible people like me to buy into things I did not really need. Many of us also cannot help jumping to conclusions about what we perceive. What I am asking parents to do here is not to go against our nature, but to be a human who strives to grow in wisdom.

We may slip up more than we like to remember. To

know that we have an emergency button is comforting. If we start to practise thinking Two-Fold during critical times to rein in our charging reactions, we could save ourselves from acting out in ways that sometimes might lead to regret or irreparable consequences.

As soon as your minds shift to think, this too has its second fold, you have immediately pulled yourself back from charging ahead in full speed to act out of reflex. If you can shift your thinking to what could give you peace of mind in the long run, you have given yourself a chance to pause in that moment. You have availed yourself of a chance to consider alternative responses. It is just like a child who is about to hit someone when you remind him that he has options. This may sound far-fetched but seriously that was how my parents taught us when we were little. They always used a saying, which could be translated as 'a noble person uses his tongue instead of his fist', to encourage us to resolve a conflict using intellect instead of violence. In order to come up with the right words on our tongue, we force our mind to switch to a different part of our brain to engage in higher order thinking.

When we train our minds to think 'hang on, what is behind this fold?' we allow ourselves a space to take a deep breath and take a step back. Train your brain to pause just like you've been trained to slam your foot on the brake in that millisecond when you perceive danger. Perchance you would be saved from over-reacting in that very instant.

When Two-Fold is used as an emergency brake we may very well hold back from uttering a regretful word or acting out. Some mistakes can be amended easily. Some are difficult to amend and may stay with us forever. These regrets can tug on our conscience, negatively affecting our ultimate wellbeing.

What follows the Two-Fold is Double-Selection. It is aimed at helping us to make better choices. More precisely, it helps us choose responses which are more conducive to our wellbeing in the long term.

Double-Selection

Double-Selection offers an alternative in decision-making; it is an alternative to your knee-jerk reaction at the time you encounter something.

The immediate desire is the first selection. We have an urge to act on what we see and feel in that very moment of encounter. For example, you see an empty seat when you hop on a bus; your first selection is to take that seat. But when you notice a fair few passengers standing you decide to find out why that seat is left vacant. You now have shifted from wanting to sit down to assessing the situation quickly. You do this to decide your course of action. This is when you enter into the process of the second selection. In those few seconds you would have gathered some information to help you make your second selection. You may find that it is a seat reserved for those more in need of it. In this case you assess your own situation and decide if you belong to that category. You may also find that the seat is dirty and you too would choose to stand.

Here is a breakdown of this process:

First fold: You see an empty seat on the bus

First selection: You want to take that seat

Second fold: You see others standing. You want to

know why. You proceed to gather clues to inform your actual choice of action

Second selection options:

1. You decide to sit down because you have a sore knee; or,
2. You decide not to sit because you are young and healthy and like others, you too want to reserve that seat for someone more deserving; or,
3. You decide to leave that seat vacant because it is dirty

This is a very simple example to walk you through the Two-Fold Double-Selection process. I hope that Omar's true story below will help you understand this concept further.

Omar's Double-Selection

I cannot use the term 'Double-Selection' without acknowledging its source. It was given to me by one of the participants in my research on parenting Muslims for my Master's dissertation.[41] A young man in his mid-twenties by the pseudonym of Omar Ahmed used what he called 'Double-Selection' to help him make his choices as an early adolescent new to Australia.

Omar was the third child of five siblings who migrated to Australia with their mother. At the time he was eleven years old.

As a single parent, Mrs. Ahmed exerted her utmost to ensure her children's education and sound character, especially after her children experienced very disrupted schooling prior to their migration due to civil war in her country.

Mrs. Ahmed, despite the language barrier, made effort to connect with her children. She sought to understand what was happening in her children's lives. She would ask about lessons they learnt at school, or activities their friends invited them to participate. She attended every child's parent-teacher night. She visited their teachers regularly to make sure they were on track with their behaviour and studies. This had a tremendous influence on Omar's decision making.

Omar recalled a time when his mum queried some black wristbands he was wearing. His mother just asked what they were and why people wore them. Omar had no idea. He said his friends gave them to him and he wore them because his friends wore them. His mother mentioned to him that certain things and activities could mean something in other people's beliefs or cultures, just like they had their own practices that meant something to them.

Omar noticed each time his mother questioned him about something it would likely be a time when he needed to make his decision using what he called the Double-Selection process. He would consider what he desired. He would also try to find out what it was about, what was involved and he would weigh it against his culture and family values.

Omar took his mother's responses as his cue. Anything that his mother questioned or refrained from commenting on would be something that he would rather stay away; even though his first selection might have been to follow what his friends did. He knew that any activity that was praiseworthy, his mother would support him, and that usually made him feel at peace.

Watering the Roots

Omar's Double-Selection process meant that he always measured his own desire against his mother's yardstick to help him choose. Some decisions were straightforward while some others required careful deliberation. Mrs. Ahmed's query in her own reserved manner afforded Omar the space to choose for himself. In order to honour this freedom, Omar, from early on, developed a taste of what it felt like to have his mother's blessing. He always chose to err on the side of caution to attain peace in his heart. Omar took his mother's response to guide him through his Double-Selection process.

Omar's Double-Selection process stood him among the ranks of those who chose their parents' blessings over their own desires. What were a few black wristbands, or going to the movies, or doing what his peers did compared to how contented he felt knowing that his mother was pleased with him? Despite having years of schooling to catch up he excelled at his studies. At the time I interviewed Omar, he was enrolled in a PhD program at the top university in his state. In his free time he led other youths in his community to fundraise for those in need. He had this calmness about him that few young people his age possessed. His Double-Selection process facilitated for him success and contributed to his wellbeing.

Now for a dissection on the example of Omar's black wristbands using Two-Fold, Double-Selection, we see how Omar's mother sowed the seed of looking behind the first fold.

First fold: Omar's friend gave him some wristbands

First selection: Omar wore them, he wanted to fit in

Second fold: Omar's mother asked why people wore

these bands. She explained they could mean something specific in other people's cultures

Second selection: Omar chose his mother's pleasure over imitating his peers. It meant more to him. Omar's Double-Selection gave him peace in his heart

Hassan, in the next story, demonstrates how acting on impulse negatively impacted his wellbeing, and how applying Two-Fold, Double-Selection helped Hassan deal with the experience.

Hassan's Experience

A dear friend of mine, Hassan, once shared with me an experience that left him feeling troubled for weeks after the encounter. Hassan was visiting a city he was not too familiar with when one night he was invited by his uncle to a dinner party at a restaurant. He hailed a taxi and asked the driver if he knew the restaurant and the driver replied in the affirmative. After some driving around the driver could not find the restaurant. Hassan called the host to tell the driver the exact location. The driver drove around some more but seeing they were getting nowhere Hassan decided to get another cab.

Already frustrated because so much time was wasted, Hassan told the driver that he was not going to pay him. The driver began to argue with him. Hassan still refused. At that point, the driver uttered, 'If you don't pay me now, we will settle the account in the Hereafter!' This was possibly the worst statement a Muslim could say to a fellow Muslim.

In our faith, we believe no one is sinless. On the Day

of Judgement every person will be recompensed for what he/she has done, i.e. good deeds will be rewarded and bad deeds punished. Acting unjustly against another person is a grave sin. When it comes to settling scores between two persons, not even God will intervene. On that Day, the oppressor will be made to pay back the oppressed from his good deeds; if he has none, the oppressed gets to dump some of his sins on the oppressor so he will receive the punishment equivalent to the weight of his oppression of the oppressed.

The driver's words stopped Hassan in his tracks. Hassan thought it was unfair of the driver to ask for payment when he did not deliver what he was hired for. Although still angry, Hassan paid the driver a small amount and asked him to leave. Grudgingly, the driver left.

Weeks went by. The driver's words still weighed heavily on Hassan's conscience. He turned the event over in his head many times questioning whether he acted unjustly to the driver? While the driver asked for fair treatment, Hassan also wanted nothing less.

Without him realising, Hassan actually went through the Two-Fold Double-Selection process. It looks like this:

First fold: The taxi driver failed to deliver that which he was hired for

First selection: Hassan refused to pay

Second fold: The driver's harsh words served as a sobering reminder for Hassan to think again in terms of the long term consequences of his action

Second selection: Although reluctant, Hassan sent the driver away with a small amount of payment

It could have been the end of it had Hassan felt justified

for his decision. However, it seemed that Hassan's second selection did not serve him as well because his heart was unsettled.

I shared my Two-Fold Double-Selection concept with Hassan. I posed the question to him: 'If someone had pulled you back in that moment, and told you to think "how should I respond in a way that is more pleasing to God?" would you have responded differently then?' Hassan went deep in thought for a while then he replied, 'I probably would. Part of me would probably still feel it was unfair that I should have to pay for two cabs. But if I had thought of it as a test to respond well, I would consider paying a few extra dollars to give me peace of mind. A few extra dollars in this life is nothing compared to having to settle the matter with him in the Hereafter. His failing to take me to my destination was a shortfall on his part but I should have negotiated with him to come to an agreement that was fair to both of us. I was pressed for time and too caught up in my anger and frustration. I wish I had known this concept to snap out of that mind frame I was in.'

Hassan knew the chance of finding that driver to make amends was a near impossibility. Using the Two-Fold, Double-Selection concept, Hassan made a different choice of action. He decided to pray for the driver and his family and to give charity on his behalf. His process is broken down as follows:

First fold: Hassan's unsettling heart over the event

First selection: He still felt he should not have to pay for a service not delivered

Second fold: Hassan realised there was a lesson behind this event from which he could learn. It was a test for him to remember his one-way journey home. He evaluated what was more important to him: his right or his peace of mind

Second selection: He did not want this matter to be settled in the Hereafter. He decided to err on the side of caution. He chose to pray for the driver and to give charity on his behalf

Hassan realised that the hidden message behind that incident was for him to cast his vision from the here and now to long-term peace and happiness. He learnt that he had an emergency brake and in future he would try to think Two-Fold, to remind himself to do what is more pleasing to God rather than to act on his impulse.

Recapitulation

In Two-Fold, we dig deeper into what is apparent. We look behind the apparently 'good'. We observe and we reflect. We direct our attention to the One in charge of the apparently good. He is the one who provides and ordains; so to Him we express our appreciation.

As for the apparently 'bad', we remind ourselves it is a test, and we are thankful that the test is not worse than it is. We try to do better than acting on impulse. When we reflect on our experiences, we see the silver lining to the dark cloud in a difficult encounter, and we will always appreciate the character-building process from the tough times in hindsight.

The Two-Fold practice gives us vision and depth in what we encounter. Practising the Two-Fold concept connects us to our inner being, keeps our curiosity alive, and most of all, helps us to be more grateful.

Thinking Two-Fold avails us of the space to accept, to submit, to appreciate; or, to let go, to prioritise, or to choose the permanent over the temporary. Everything except our Creator is transient. This is because, 'whatever you have will end, what God has is lasting. And We will surely give those who were patient their reward, according to the best of what they used to do'.[42] Therefore applying the Two-Fold guideline is one way to channel our concern and focus on the Everlasting. Only by doing so, is attaining true wellbeing possible.

The Double-Selection process helps us choose what matters more to us over what our ego desires in that moment. We forego the transient for what is permanent. We learn to trust in the One who knows what is ultimately good for us. The Most Generous Lord will surely reward those who are patient in striving to do the right thing by Him.

If we are able to internalise this way of thinking, and intentionally put it into practice, we open ourselves to perceive more than what is apparent. We allow ourselves the opportunity to make better choices in alignment with our principles and values.

Development of wellbeing in this book differs from contemporary work on wellbeing in that we orient our thinking from our apparent perceptions to the subtle, from the great to the Greater, from the creation to its Creator. We make choices less out of whim and more out of what is better in the long term. This is helpful because as discussed in the previous chapter, we are journeying home. We may become distracted momentarily from time to time; but we are less likely to get stuck at any one point along our journey, whether it appears 'good' or otherwise.

Hardship and challenges happen for a purpose. Look beyond the apparent. Surely only through experiencing bitterness one notices the subtle sweetness that one cannot understand through any other way. How true is it that we deepen our appreciation for health after we have experienced sickness? Having a habit to be mindful of the Two-Fold nature of things and make sound choices using Double-Selection keeps our minds open and reins in our impulses.

Parenteers are highly recommended to incorporate this component into their lives. Life is guaranteed to throw up challenges at you. Children are most definitely going to push you to your limits. Children who witness adults practising the Two-Fold, Double-Selection process have a better chance to adopt the same approach later in their own lives.

This concludes the current discussion on the Two-Fold, Double-Selection component of the 1-2-3 Wellbeing Guide. The third component, Three-Way Connection, consists of three elements: Inward, Vertical and External Connections. The next chapter offers an overview of the Three-Way Connection component before each element is subsequently explained in detail in their respective chapters.

CHAPTER FIVE
Wellbeing Guide Third Component:

THREE-WAY CONNECTION AT A GLANCE

> *... and unless they hold fast to a lifeline from God and from mankind, they are overshadowed by vulnerability wherever they are found*[43]

THIS QUR'ANIC VERSE sums up the third component of the Wellbeing Guide. The three ways are: connect with oneself inwardly, connect vertically with one's Creator, and connect outwardly with everything external that one encounters. This chapter sketches a brief overview of what they are and why they are important. A separate chapter has been dedicated to discussing each connection in more depth from Chapters Six to Eight respectively.

Inward Connection

This connection is all about knowing your inner self and managing your emotions, your innermost thoughts and internal dialogues you have with yourself. It helps you to understand your human-ness, getting to know yourself in terms of your natural disposition, the structure of the soul, and managing the constant struggle between the various states of the nafs (soul).

The fitrah, or the natural disposition of the human, from an Islamic viewpoint, is that everyone is born with 'the same sound nature which most agreed is pure and which comes from and has a direct link to God'.[44] It is also human nature to become attracted and attached to this worldly life. As humans live through life on Earth, this pure nature is distanced and covered due to a process of corruption.[45]

This seemingly conflicting personality within us is based on Imam al-Ghazali's theory on human psychology. In his seminal work, *The Revival of the Religious Sciences (Ihya' Ulumuddeen)*[46], Imam al-Ghazali discusses three principle states of the nafs. These are: the inciting nafs (nafs al-ammaarah),[47] the self-reproaching nafs (nafs al-lawwamah),[48] and the nafs at peace (nafs al-mutmainnah).[49] Ahmet Tanhan explains the different states of the nafs as similar to that of aspects of the nafs on a spectrum.[50] The human nafs 'moves back and forth on the spectrum based on one's thoughts, attitudes, intentions and actions.'[51]

In addition to the nature and structure of our inner self, Rothman and Coyle's theoretical categories of the soul also include the structure of the soul and development of the soul[52] which are found to be very helpful in learning how best to manage ourselves.

The Islamic perspective on human psychology proposes that the human hearts are always in a tug-of-war between our attraction towards the worldly pleasures and our desire to achieve the everlasting pleasures in the Hereafter. People struggle between right and wrong, and between inclining towards evil and feeling remorseful afterwards.[53] A snippet of the three principle states of the nafs is presented in the following paragraphs.

The Inciting Nafs (Nafs Al-Ammarah)

The inciting nafs is a state of human's lower self, including a person's basic instincts. Of all the struggles of human experience, striving to keep one's inciting nafs under control in order to obey God is the most difficult.[54] This state of the nafs is attracted to animalistic gratifications. It loves materialistic possessions and sensual pleasures. It is easily inclined towards selfishness, self-indulgence and heedlessness of God. The inclination to individuation pulls the person downward and has a tendency to respond to Satan's promptings towards evil.

Letting the inciting nafs run wild leads to destruction of the person. The animalist aspect of the nafs shares the instinct of other animals in the animal kingdom for food, warmth, security and sex. The inciting nafs also has the potential to debase a person's soul to worse than that of an animal. This level of the nafs has a tendency to subject itself to the whisperings and promptings of the Satan and his army. Thus are the references to one who wrongs his own soul in the Qur'an.[55]

The environment in which we are brought up, the company we keep, and our worldviews all play a part in our level of awareness and how we manage our inciting nafs. Like a child, we can train the nafs to behave well or we can let it fester into a monster. An unrestrained nafs follows its relentless desires like a bottomless pit. This is why Frager translates Nafs Al-Ammarah as the *tyrannical nafs* because it 'attempts to dominate us and to control our thoughts and actions.'[56] This nafs can easily become a tool for Satan's evil promptings.[57]

When the inciting nafs takes control of a person, one develops traits such as greed, laziness, vanity, arrogance, jealousy, hatred, miserliness, heedlessness and so on. These traits are detrimental to a person's wellbeing.

Fortunately for us, the Creator has placed in us another aspect of nafs, the self-reproaching nafs, that checks on and questions the human's inner thoughts and actions.

The Self-Reproaching Nafs (Nafs Al-Lawwamah)

The self-reproaching or regretful nafs is inspired by the heart. Frager explains, 'The sense of the Arabic word lawwama[h] is that of resisting wrongdoing and asking God's forgiveness after we become conscious of wrongdoing'.[58] I understand its role is like a police and judge rolled into one to check on our intents and behaviour. It is the conscience that raises red flags to make us question our thoughts and actions.

Here is the question: What must we do with our nafs? On one hand we have an inciting nafs that is inclined towards pleasurable indulgence and sins, while on the other hand we have a self-reproaching nafs that keeps us on our toes, to make us feel bad about our wrongdoings. In Sufi teachings, understanding this about ourselves is a first step. It helps us realise our dependency on our Creator, and it motivates us to ask for guidance, to engage in purification of our nafs, and to aspire towards higher states of our being.

I am a strong advocate for Muslim parents to learn about human nature and tendencies from Islamic psychology. Knowledge on our soul provides an important foundation to teach children to exercise self-control, and to self-regulate, because our hearts were born to reflect the Divine light. Parents have a vital role in training our children to understand and train their nafs. More discussion on Inward Connection will be presented in Chapter Six.

Through the endless tug-of-war between our inciting nafs and self-reproaching nafs, we aspire to get to the state of nafs at peace (nafs al-mutmainnah), or the peaceful self, to be described next in brief.

The Soul At Peace (**Nafs Al-Mutmainnah**)

This is a state when the human heart is at complete peace and contentment. Very few attain this state of nafs. It is possible to gain moments of that state. It is nevertheless a state worth striving for anyone who desires to live for a higher purpose. Moreover, it is a state in which one will be allowed to enter the eternal Paradise by the mercy of God. An illustration of what the nafs will experience in this state can be seen in the following verse in the Qur'an when the nafs is told: 'you soul at peace: return to your Lord well pleased and well pleasing; go in among My servants; and into My Garden!'[59]

God has repeatedly sent messengers to urge and teach mankind ways to live for a higher purpose in our worldly existence for a blissful eternity in the Hereafter. The life on Earth we have now is our opportunity to put in our best effort while we still can. Pursuit of this ultimate wellbeing positively impacts on our existence in every dimension of our wellbeing.

This is a quick introduction on the first part of the Three-Way Connection, which is Inward Connection, or connecting to our inner self. Now let us look at the second part of the connection, that is, to connect ourselves vertically with our Creator.

Vertical Connection

Vertical connection is the connection we actively seek with the One who is in charge of everything in the universe—our Lord, Creator and Sustainer of all that exists. Vertical Connection is the channel through which we look after our holistic wellbeing. It is the central axis to our holistic wellbeing. Through this connection we learn to read the map to keep us on track.

Those of us who have ever moved houses will agree that one of the first things we have to do when we move into a new place is to connect utilities such as electricity, gas, telephone and internet services to our new dwelling. Without these services, our life will be very difficult. Suppose there were one number we could call that switched on all facilities we needed, and to this one account we paid all our bills, and it was also this number we dialled for repairs or services? It would certainly make life so much easier. Vertical Connection can be likened to that one magic number.

Who Ya Gonna Call?

Who ya gonna call? For maintenance of our spiritual being, which I believe to be a key aspect that flows to all other dimensions of wellbeing, we have a hotline to call, that is, connect vertically with our Lord. It is available 24/7. As complicated as life is, there is a straightforward path for those seeking it.

It is easy. All one needs to do is to firstly recognise you want to connect with the One in charge who is infinitely greater, wiser, fairer and more powerful than all that exists. It is the One Being from whom all came into existence, upon whom everyone depends and to whom shall all return.

How do we know who this being is? The answer is—look for His consistent messages and signs that point to Him throughout the history of mankind, in our own miraculous existence and uncountable signs around us.

Revelations and messengers have consistently been sent to guide us to recognise Him, acknowledge Him, submit to and connect with Him. All monotheistic religions continuously point mankind to the same Lord.

Connecting vertically avails us of a grip in life. It decreases the chances of wandering blindly, and instead, it leads us to a straight path with a clear destination in mind. Vertical Connection joins the dots for us. It clarifies and simplifies our purpose on Earth.

How to find Him, master of the Universe? Let us look at the example of Prophet Ibrahim (peace be upon him). He followed his natural disposition and turned to the sky in search for his Lord. Firstly he took the stars, then the moon and lastly the sun as his Lord. Yet after watching each of them set, he recognised that there had to be a greater being in charge of even the most glorious of heavenly bodies. As splendid as they were when they appeared, they also set. Ibrahim used his faculties of sight and intellect to observe, to deduce, to comprehend, to finally asking for guidance from the Creator of the heavens and the earth and everything in between. He submitted to Him, the Lord of all the worlds. To symbolise this connection, I visualise this connection in a vertical direction upwards. The point of connection within us is right here in our heart.

The reality is, whether we acknowledge God or not, we live within God's system in spite of ourselves. We cannot exist without His Divine will. While all creations are dependent on Him, He is independent from anything. He only has to withdraw water or air, and all living things will perish. He only has to order the sun to come millimetres closer, and everything on Earth will burn into ashes. It is by God's will the sky is stretched above us like a canopy without anything holding it up. If He willed, the sky would come crashing down on our planet just as easily as it has been suspended above us.

It is only for our own benefit that we connect ourselves to our Creator and take heed of His guidance to live our life in a positive, healthy, productive and purposeful manner. It is as logical as following the manufacturer's instruction manual to operate an appliance or machinery. Our Lord is the only source of contentment for us. He sent down

His words as our map to guide us along our life journey. Vertical Connection is a means to a life of structure, of meaning, of satisfaction, of security and of hope.

The Lord's promise of a final hearing and sentencing on the Day of Judgment with absolute justice consoles us when we are disillusioned by injustice, tyranny, dictatorship and cruelty of all kinds. His attributes of love, fairness and power keeps us in awe and hope for His mercy. In my personal view, there can be no lasting wellbeing without Vertical Connection.

Referring to Al-Ghazali, Skellie explains that man's aptitude for submitting to the One omnipotent power other than a creation is what elevates mankind to a position of honour above all other creatures. The seat of this aptitude is found in the heart.[60]

Outward/External Connection

The third part of this Three-Way Connection is Outward/External Connection. By this I mean how we respond to and interact with external stimuli that we encounter in life. I call all of these stimuli 'external encounters'. External encounters include experiences, information, people, circumstances, opportunities, events, places, and animate and inanimate objects etc., with which we interact.

How we view the external encounters and how we respond to them according to guidelines from divine sources is what I term 'external connection'. External connection can impact our wellbeing either positively or negatively.

External encounters can fulfill our needs, appeal to our senses and desires, and as well they can be tests that devastate or harm our existence. Our inciting nafs is attracted to glitters of the material world and is easily swayed by the promptings of devils.

Certain encounters are harsh and crushing (e.g. tsunamis, earthquakes, drought, flood, illnesses, tragic loss of loved ones) while others are heart-warming and exhilarating (kind people, beautiful nature etc.). Some encounters are appealing to our inciting nafs but their harm outweigh their benefits (e.g., gambling and alcohol).

The challenge of external connection lies in discerning right from wrong, to effectively manage our needs and wants. Further discussions of the external connection will be presented in Chapter Eight.

The Interconnectedness Of The Three-Way Connection

While inward connection focuses on knowing our inner selves and managing our emotions and thoughts, the outward connection is about choosing our responses to external encounters. Vertical connection provides us with a map to guide and enhance our connections internally and externally.

Mere knowledge about external encounters does not necessarily result in enhanced wellbeing. Two examples are cigarette smoking and regular exercise. There is abundant education and evidence available on the health hazards of cigarette smoking and a sedentary lifestyle. The majority of people who continue to reach for their next cigarette or procrastinate for another day on the couch do so in spite of their knowledge. Knowledge alone does not give us immunity against our inciting nafs. Knowledge must be followed by consistent action. Repeated actions result in the establishment of habits. Good habits contribute to our wellbeing. In our human-ness, given our tendencies, we are in need of guidance and consistent intentional action to strive for our ultimate wellbeing.

The human heart being the receptacle of guidance needs regular maintenance in order to respond appropriately to Divine guidance. Just as mirrors need regular dusting and wiping, our hearts need purification to reflect Divine light. To prepare the heart to reflect light, one needs to implement instructions from the maker of hearts. Our spiritual wellbeing is maintained through regular engagement in introspection, sincere acts of worship, repentance, charity, and praiseworthy deeds. One will find that whenever one chooses to obey God over one's own whims and desires one becomes the ultimate beneficiary. This is what I call 'closing the loop' through external encounters for wellbeing.

In summary, the Three-Way Connection allows a person to interact with the external encounters from a place of humility within oneself through one's regular connection vertically. Frequent remembrance of God, regular acts of worship and good deeds cleanse our heart to respond to guidance. Guidance opens the gateway for us to attain ultimate wellbeing, starting from sincere intention through how we interact with the external encounters in life.

Parents who seek to understand the natural disposition of the soul and its attraction to this worldly life, its structure and the fluctuating states of the nafs, are in a better position to help a child develop his/her character and to make sound choices for themselves. The three chapters following this chapter discusses each part of the Three-Way Connections in detail.

CHAPTER SIX
Inward Connection

If we could see our shadow (the dark side of our nature), we should be immune to any moral and mental infection and insinuation.[61]

I KNOW A STUDENT who battled with guilt and low self-worth. From an outsider's perspective, this young person had everything going for him. He excelled in his studies. He came from a good family. He had many talents. Yet he suffered from anxiety and at times, depression. He never lived in the moment. When he studied, he wished he could play. When he played, he was plagued by guilt concerning studies he should have been doing. He spent his energy beating himself up over what he 'ought' to be doing instead. He felt unproductive. He experienced fatigue. He was forever chasing the 'should've-s', 'could've-s' and 'ought to be-s' in his head. Eventually he went for professional help.

The above example is not an isolated incident. Anxiety, depression and suicide are the most prevalent mental disorders affecting young people. There are 25.1% of young people between the age of thirteen and eighteen years affected by anxiety disorders according to the Anxiety and Depression Association of America.[62] In Australia, one in six young people between twelve and seventeen years of age experience anxiety.[63] According to the Telethon Kids Institute:

> Levels of anxiety higher than what can be expected of children's age and development can negatively impact with their ability to do what other children and adolescents their age do. Nearly half of all children with a mental disorder experience an anxiety disorder.[64]

Let alone young people, how many adults know what is happening within themselves? I was first introduced to Imam Al-Ghazali's (1052–1111) work on Islamic psychology through a series of lesson on diseases of the heart. A few years later I took another course and gained better understanding of Imam Al-Ghazali's analysis and analogies of the human psyche. It gave me a much-needed framework with which to understand myself, my decisions, my desires, the internal conflicts, the good intentions as well as the bad. Prior to that I felt like I was operating this sophisticated machine called 'self' blindly, without knowledge of its design and functions of its parts. Imam Al-Ghazali's explanation on the four structures, or faculties, namely, the rooh (spirit), the nafs (soul), the qalb (heart) and the 'aql (intellect)[65]; what the firtah (nature of the nafs) is; how the nafs gets influenced; what to watch out for and how to manage ourselves were eye-opening.

I cannot help but ask myself why was something as vital as this not taught to me as a child, or as a youth growing up? I consider this knowledge essential to everyone, especially parents. This chapter is presented in two sections. The first section introduces readers to a perspective of the human self from Al-Ghazali's work. The second section offers a number of practices to enhance personal wellbeing.

Section I: Perspective Of Human Self From Islamic Psychology

Rothman and Coyle's theoretical categories of the soul based on Al-Ghazali's framework of human psychology have made it easy for us to better understand the makeup and dynamics of our inner selves. The following sub-sections explain three of the four main categories of the soul: nature of the soul, structure of the soul, and states of the soul. The fourth category is development of the soul, of which the authors put forth a number of subcategories through which one may work towards purification and refinement.

The Nature Of The Soul

The nature of nafs is called fitrah (natural disposition) in Arabic. Unlike the belief in original sin, Muslims believe that every child is born with a pure soul and a fitrah 'that signifies human's inborn, intuitive ability to discern between right and wrong, true and false, and to sense God's existence and oneness.'[66] This is our in-built compass that connects us with our Creator. To worship God is a human's natural disposition.

Rothman and Coyle explain that although 'we may be out of touch with our knowledge of and witnessing of God, but we always have the ability to get back to it.'[67]

The understanding that humans having both tendencies towards good and evil is not new. The following is a Cherokee story to which these tendencies of the human self was inferred:

> One evening the old Cherokee told his grandson about a battle that goes on inside people. He said, 'My son, the battle is between two wolves inside us all. One is Evil. It is anger, envy, jealousy, sorrow, regret, greed, arrogance, self-pity, guilt, resentment, inferiority, lies, false pride, superiority and ego.
>
> The other is Good. It is joy, peace, love, hope, serenity, humility, kindness, benevolence, empathy, generosity, truth, compassion and faith.'
>
> The grandson thought about it for a minute and then asked his grandfather, 'Which wolf wins?'
>
> The Cherokee simply replied, 'The one you feed.'[68]

This story indicates that in other cultures people also believe human's capability of choosing between good and evil; the more we lean towards one, the stronger that 'wolf' becomes.

The Structure Of The Soul
The Rooh (Pure Spirit)

As explained in Chapter Two, our rooh (spirit) was created long before we came into being. This is the origin of our fitrah. Our rooh had already acknowledged the Lordship of our Creator. The evidence is found in the following verse in the Qur'an:

> ... when your Lord took from Adam's children, from their [very] loins, their offspring and made them bear witness about themselves, He said, 'Am I not your Lord?' and they replied, 'Yes, we bear witness.'...[69]

Then came our physical being, beginning with fertilisation of a sperm and ovum, to developing into a fully formed foetus ready for life in this physical world in approximately 40 weeks. As mentioned in Chapter Two, at around 120 days the rooh is blown into the foetus.[70]

We know very little about the rooh. God says in the Qur'an, '[Prophet], they ask you about the Spirit. Say, "The Spirit is part of my Lord's domain. You have only been given a little knowledge..."'[71] What concerns us presently is our nafs in our physical existence.

The Nafs (Soul or Self)

Our physical being is formed by basic molecules such as carbon, hydrogen and oxygen that also make up other creations. The appearances and shapes of different creatures are mere variations in arrangement of the basic building blocks. That said, humans stand out from the rest of the creations because there is a unique aspect within the human which makes us capable of selecting our courses of action for higher purposes. This is the nafs (soul) that resides within the heart. It is incorporeal and subtle. At birth, the nafs is activated like the flick of a switch to make it possible for the human to live in this physical world. The body is like a jacket that encases our nafs. According to Dharamsi and Maynard[72] the nafs can be explained in terms of one's persona, or self that gives a person's personality, emotions, temperament, decisions, desires etc.

The Qalb (The Heart)

Prophet Muhammad (peace and blessings be upon him) refers to the heart as 'a morsel of flesh which, if it be whole, all the body is whole and which, if it be diseased, all of it is diseased. Truly it is the heart'.[73] The heart to which the Prophet is referring is not the organ with its physiological functions. The Hadith states that the heart can be sound or it can become corrupted. It does more than the muscle that pumps blood to our blood vessels. Rather it is the heart of hearts—the essence in us that makes us human. The heart is the term used by Islamic as well as Jewish and Christian religious scholars and philosophers for the 'seat of intellectual and emotional life'. This aspect of the heart is what Imam Al-Ghazali calls the 'seat of knowing and perceiving, experiencing'.[74]

The heart is where intangible essences of human such as knowledge, ideas, memory, emotions, desires etc. are contained. The heart to the body is like the driver's seat to a vehicle. The soundness of the person's heart very much depends on who we allow to occupy the driver's seat.

The 'Aql (The Mind)

The 'aql is the intelligence or mind in a human. Sheikh Mokhtar Maghraoui pointed out an interesting fact that the word 'aql has only appeared in the Qur'an in its verb form as in 'being actively aware of something, being in restraint and restraining and controlling…'.[75] From this we understand that the various forms of the word 'aql in the Qur'an are more about the mind's purpose than the entity itself. Like the word processor, we are focused on its processing ability than the tool itself.

The functional ability of mind consists of receiving, analysing, remembering, interpreting, extrapolating and expanding knowledge that elevates human beings above all other creations. Hence the 'aql is a tool to be used with care. It is undoubtedly the most superior tool given to creations. Yet the heart that uses the tool wisely is what really sets humans apart from the rest of the creations. An evil heart that uses the 'aql for selfish, demonic purposes cannot compare with an angelic heart that uses the 'aql for praiseworthy causes. God reveals in the Qur'an:

> We created man in the finest state; then reduced him to the lowest of the low but those who believe and do good deeds will have an unfailing reward. After this, what makes you deny the Judgement? Is God not the most decisive of judges?[76]

Which human is wicked enough to be degraded to the lowest of the low? The answer is those who despite being honoured with the status of human, choose to ignore the signs, the reminders and admonishment sent down by God. They use their intellect, a tool, to pursue what their animalistic, beastly, or demonic natures desire. In doing so they stoop to the level of the demon, the animal or the beast. Rather, they render themselves lower than the lowest because they choose to misuse their honourable capability. The animals and the beasts were not endowed with the faculty to choose and therefore they have not been given the status among creations as the humans have.

In contrast, those who choose to be honoured by their Creator are in fact higher than the angels because they need to exert effort to fight back all human tendencies towards temptations while angels were created to obey. Angels obey by nature not by choice.

States Or Stages Of The Soul

Abu Musa reported that the Prophet said, 'The parable of the heart is that of a feather blown about by the wind of the desert.'[77] This Hadith tells us that the human heart changes frequently. In other words, it can be easily swayed.

As outlined in Chapter Five, Al-Ghazali writes about three principle states of nafs. These are the inciting nafs, the reproaching nafs and the nafs at peace.

The Inciting Nafs (Nafs Al-Ammarah)

The inciting nafs pulls the heart towards one's base desires. Its primary function is to help mankind to survive. The inciting nafs nudges us to eat food; without which we would starve to death. The inciting nafs dislikes pain, so it puts us on high alert to avoid pain. The inciting nafs loves to rest, and sleep helps us restore our energy.

However, if left untethered, this state of nafs overtakes

the heart to indulge in actions that satisfy the animal, the beast and the demon in us. Satan works on those who have a stronger tendency to obey their inciting nafs in order to commit excess and transgress. The inciting nafs that often gets the upper hand would command the person to indulge in whatever he desires. An indulgent person dislikes the virtue of moderation, and seeks easy ways out in the face of difficulties. They tend to settle for idleness, attracted to vanity and greed, desire power and excessive luxury, neglectful and heedless of their Creator, and are prone to addiction and substances abuse.

The Reproaching Nafs (Nafs Al-Lawwamah)

Since we are inherently connected to our Creator and therefore have been equipped with an internal compass called fitrah (natural disposition), we have a natural need to connect to our Creator and an innate sense of right and wrong. Our reproaching nafs alerts us when we intend, see or do wrong. This is the inner voice that says, 'I don't feel good about this', or 'that seems wrong to me!' or 'I shouldn't have done that!' It pulls you back a fraction, and causes you to pause from your impulses and reconsider your intention and actions. Regret motivates you to find a way to atone for your wrong actions. This is your reproaching nafs at play. We all have it in us. However, repeatedly silencing the reproaching nafs only leaves the gateway wide open to embolden the inciting nafs.

Satan hones in on human weaknesses. If a human being sins, Satan wins. If Satan cannot incite a person to sin, then he tries his darnedest to stop him from doing the right thing.

The most desired state to strive for, is the self at peace (nafs al mutmainnah).

The Nafs at Peace (Nafs Al-Mutmainnah)

Much work is required to obtain this state, which provides a path for one to work for a blessed existence both in this life and in the Hereafter. Positive psychology holds that certain mindsets and practices can help us improve our state of wellbeing. In other words, if we know what makes up our inner self, when combined with conscious practices, we can improve our wellbeing. The Wellbeing Guide in this book aims to help us develop this state of nafs.

The Four Inclinations Of Nafs

Imam Al-Ghazali saw the dynamics of human nafs at play and he acknowledged that each of these tendencies exists in us for a specific purpose. He uses metaphors to demonstrate how some aspects of the human nafs require nurturing, some aspects are to be vigilantly resisted, while other aspects are to be contained, but not completely denied. According to Imam Al-Ghazali the human nafs comes with four tendencies—the animal, the beast, the demon and the angel.[78]

The Animal

It is built within us to have biological needs. The basic biological needs such as eating, drinking, sleeping and copulating are also present in other creations in the animal kingdom. This aspect of human nature is essential for our survival in this physical world, therefore complete denial of this nature leads to our own demise. Moderation in these activities is the key to sustaining a healthy physical existence. Overindulgence in any aspect of our animalistic nature is detrimental to our wellbeing. Shamelessness, greed, impurity, meanness, miserliness are some examples of negative traits that develop as a result of one letting his animalistic nature extend beyond its limits.

The Beast

Anger is a manifestation of this tendency in us. The beast can be helpful for self-protection. However, like fire, if left to rage without restraint, this nature is destructive to the self and others. When turned inward, one develops feelings of worthlessness and self-hatred. When expressed outwardly, this tendency can be manifested as violence and brutality. Imam Al-Ghazali writes, 'If he [a person] obeys the dictates of anger, he acquires heinous conducts such as haughtiness, pride, love of power, self-praise, jokes, contempt for others, oppression.'[79] A person who channels his beastly tendency towards a good cause develops qualities such as heroism, kindness and patience.

The Demon

This is the deceptive tendency in humans. This aspect of human nature is a test for human beings. We have been warned over and over in the Qur'an to be on guard against the deceptions and tricks of the Satan. Satan alone cannot succeed in acts of murder, rape, fraud, or destruction. He needs a vehicle to carry out his evil. His accomplice is the demonic tendency of the human nafs. He knows humans have the sharpest tools, namely, the intellect, the passion, the will, and also the ability to manipulate, deceive and plot. The demonic nature within humans is Satan's contact point to materialise his evil.

Satan, being one of human's external encounters, is forever sitting in wait for any opportunity to incite humans to sin. Satan's evil promptings escape no one. This is why humans are prone to sin. Those who let their demonic nature take control of his existence are the ones who have formed a strong alliance with Satan. This nature, if allowed to carry on unrestrained, will misuse the intellect to one's demonic pursuits. Remembrance of God, regular repentance and performing good deeds to atone for one's sins allow for one's heart to be protected and purified.

The Angel

This is the part of the human nature that aspires to purity. It yearns to return to its origin in heaven, where the pure rooh's eternal home is. If one is able to control the animalistic, the beastly and the demonic tendencies mentioned above, his heart would be receptive to light. An illuminated heart is endowed with wisdom and knowledge. He develops virtues of humility, compassion, forgiveness, contentment, self-satisfaction, self-discipline, God-consciousness and modesty.

The angel in us desires the Hereafter, eternity, and being close to our Creator. When our nafs is free from attachment to this world, and its focus is shifted to serving our Creator, our nafs is in a state of tranquillity, or nafs at peace (nafs al-mutmainnah). To attain this state of peace, one needs to follow the divine guidance, to detach from the material world and to purify the soul.

Points For Discussion

Recognise The Struggle

I visualise the demonic and angelic tendencies as two ends of a see-saw, if one is up, the other is down, all the while the animal and the beast are running around that can knock the see-saw off its balance. Since human beings are not completely angelic nor are they completely demonic, all humans struggle between these two tendencies throughout their life. This is what the Evil and Good that the old Cherokee grandfather in the story was referring to. Which aspect of our nature gains the upper hand depends on which one we feed. If the needs of our nafs are neglected, with the exception of the demon, we become unwell. If left to indulge, the animal and the beast can easily team up with the demonic traits that opens the gate for Satan's cunning to pull us down to a state of utter debasement. The good news is, the animal and the beast can be trained and restrained. The demon in us is the one against which we need to guard with vigilance. Even better news is that Islam offers every solution to help the angel in us to win the battle so our souls can return to the eternal abode in the best possible state we can. That state is the state of a peaceful soul (nafs al-mutmainnah).

In the current era of information, human beings have reached heights never before achieved in terms of scientific and technological advancements. The world, on the other hand, has never experienced such destructive effects of these advancements which have come from humans' 'intelligence'. Reliance purely on the mind without divine guidance has led the world to 'advance' to an unconscionable state never before witnessed in the history of mankind. Global warming, acid rain, severe drought, resource depletion and genetically modified organisms are just some examples of the consequences of misusing the mind. While there is little we can do to stop or reverse the damage already being done, we each still can choose to do the right thing within our capacity, if not for saving the world, at least to save our conscience. This is the central theme of this book—to keep the bigger picture in mind in order to make the right choices for a peaceful heart.

Know Your Blueprint

To attain success in this life and in the Hereafter one needs to take care of the various natures of his nafs. Prophet Muhammad (peace and blessings be upon him) said, 'All of the children of Adam are sinners, and the best sinners are those who repent.'[80] This is because human beings are weak. We easily give in to temptations and ideas appealing to the animal, the beast or the demon in us. One way to redeem ourselves is through sincere repentance.

The Creator has been informing mankind through His chain of prophets and divine revelations to His chosen messengers to help those who wish to follow His guidance to attain success.

> Prosperous are those who purify themselves, remember the name of their Lord, and pray. Yet

you [people] prefer the life of this world, even though the Hereafter is better and more lasting. All this is in the earlier scriptures, the scriptures of Abraham and Moses.[81]

The most accurate instruction manual of any appliance is the one that comes from its manufacturer. The most applicable version of any book is the latest edition. The most trustworthy knowledge of ourselves and of the Hereafter has to come from the One who created us. The Qur'an is the final revelation of God which confirms all that was sent before it.

Knowing our nature is like having the blueprint of our inner self in view. If it is common sense for a mechanic to know the ins and outs of a vehicle in order to carry out his work, how about parents who are raising another human being? To me learning about our inner self from Islamic psychology has been the single most vital piece of knowledge that guided me to work towards attaining peace with myself. It gave me the courage to face my own shortcomings and sins. Knowing my own inclinations and how to manage myself is empowering. I cannot find the right words to explain how critical it is for parents to be equipped with this knowledge when raising a child. This is the key to understanding our own, as well as our children's motivation, behaviour, and to managing our emotions. Knowing why a child behaves a certain way is half the battle won.

Ulitlise Your Tools Wisely

Initially we relate to the world through having our basic needs met; these include food, warmth and being cared for. As we develop we learn to make sense, bit by bit, of the external encounters, and we utilise our tools, such as our senses of hearing, sight, touch, smell and taste, and our mind as well as our limbs to acquire our wants and desires. We need guidance to learn about the external encounters and to develop the ability to choose the appropriate responses to them for self-preservation and for positive growth.

Most of what appeals to us in this world is temporary. Focusing on pursuing only worldly pleasures is like running after a mirage at best, and to be deceived at worst. Take power and pain for instance. Both are related to our existence in this world. One who is addicted to power will spare no effort to acquire it. The hunger for power can overcome a person's humanity. Another person who leans on substances to numb her pain will go to any length to get her fix. Both addictions come with harmful consequences. On the other hand, kindness, charity, and giving service to others, do not come with destructive consequences. Mankind is enjoined to do more of them, with or without believing in a religion. The pleasures one gains are not tangible, and if you have faith, they extend beyond this transient life. God promised everlasting rewards to those who do good.

Decide Who Occupies The Driver's Seat

Why is it that we find it so difficult to obey God and to exercise self-control? This is because our nafs is attracted to the pomp and glitter of this material life, easily overcome by our emotions, leaving the door wide open to the whisperings of Satan. Satan and his army try hard to push either the animal or the beast in us to occupy the driver's seat so they can lead the person to execute their evil. To minimise the demonic influence over us, we need to adopt measures to moderate and restrain our animalistic and beastly tendencies.

The trickiest is the demon in us. The extent of vigilance in guarding our hearts against the demon's promptings can be likened to the way we protect our properties from thieves and deceiving schemers. We cannot afford to be complacent.

All three—the animal, the beast and the demon—can lead a person to sin and self-destruction. The animal and the beast need to be trained and put on a leash. Learning self-control and delayed gratification tames these two tendencies. The demon needs to be locked up. Remembrance of God in the forms of supplications, recitation of the Qur'an, seeking God's protection, and keeping the right company are all effective weapons to keep the demon at bay. Sins leave black marks on the heart causing the heart to obscure the light and harden until, devoid of goodness, it can no longer respond to the light from the Divine. A diseased heart makes the soul miserable, wicked and loathsome, deprived of joy or happiness.

The voice of the reproaching nafs can be likened to our conscience. When the heart is clean, divine knowledge illuminates the heart, one learns to use the 'aql (mind/intellect) like a sharp tool with caution, in obeying God. God's pleasure blesses the heart with peace and tranquillity.

Do children have the ability to exercise restraint? The answer is yes. The famous marshmallow test mentioned in Chapter Two demonstrated children's ability to delay gratification before the age of five. Children as young as two years of age have shown abilities of voluntary inhibition,[82] and by the age of five, they can become reasonably competent at regulating impulsive behaviour over extended periods of time.[83] The caregivers play a continuous and important role in facilitating a child's overall progression to self-regulation.[84]

Purification Of The Heart

God revealed to us in the Qur'an over fourteen centuries ago that naaseyat is the part of human that lying and sinning take place.[85] Naaseyat is the Arabic term for the front part of the head, or the frontal lobe.[86] It is only in recent years that this part of the brain was identified as being

> ... responsible for cognition, behaviour and emotional activity. Prefrontal cortex receives information from the limbic system (involved in emotional control) and acts as a mediator between cognition and feelings through executive functions. Executive functions are a set of cognitive skills necessary for controlling and self-regulating your behaviour.[87]

A person who lies and sins does so wilfully. The brain is therefore like an information processor. Whatever data enters the brain through the sensory gates, the processing takes place in the frontal lobe. A word processor processes information. The operator of this processor determines what data enters, and he is the one who decides what he does with the data. An illuminated heart uses the brain for praiseworthy purposes and a diseased heart uses the brain for deviant pursuits.

To keep the heart illuminated, one adopts a purification process involving two actions:

1. Guard what is allowed to pass through the sensory gates to the heart, and
2. Engage in development of the soul

The development process includes, but is not limited to, fulfilling the mandatory duties such as salat (formal prayers) siyam (fasting), zakat (paying dues to the poor), increasing voluntary forms of worship, doing good deeds and frequent practice of dhikr (remembrance of God).

To stay on track we need to ask God to help us. Anas bin Malik narrated a supplication often made by the Prophet, 'O turner of hearts, keep my heart firm on your religion.'[88]

Since it is within human nature to err, one needs to be totally honest with one's intention and behaviour to get back on track for one's heart to be aligned with the Vertical Connection as much as one can.

Can religious experiences impact a person's wellbeing positively? There is growing interest among neuroscientists and theologians in this respect. It has taken them into a fairly new field of studies named neurotheology, or spiritual neuroscience. Recent research at Utah University using neuroimaging data and behavioural self-report data to test nineteen Mormon participants observed a consistent association between spiritual experience and the activation of the nucleus accumbens and several cortical regions in the brain.[89] It is explained in this paper that the nucleus accumbens in the brain is the same region that has been observed to respond to acutely positive effects, including maternal and romantic love, appreciation of music and as a common pathway for chemically induced states of euphoria associated with drug abuse. Participants in this research experienced faster heart rates and deepened breathing during peak feelings of spirituality. This research sheds light on the positive impact of spirituality on wellbeing from a scientific viewpoint. I wonder if a child who did not receive the kindness, love and positive experiences would take addictive substitutes to experience that exhilarated feeling? If my thinking is on the right track, then parental love and assistance in connecting children vertically early on in life are indispensable in their wellbeing development.

This concludes the first section of this chapter, which took us on a tour inward using references from the Qur'an, Hadith and scholarly interpretations of spiritual psychology. The remaining section of this chapter suggests a few practices, among many, to enhance our wellbeing through connection with our inner self.

Section II: Inward Connection Practices For Wellbeing

There are many ways to connect inwardly. I would like to suggest two essential practices that are beneficial to both you and your children: self-awareness and self-care.

Self-Awareness

Among the first and most essential practices for personal growth is self-awareness. For parents in particular, this is perhaps the single most important inward connection practice to start with in order to make positive changes in our parenting.

Growing up I was trained to be considerate of others, to be polite, to be kind to others and to do the right thing for others. Without a doubt these are all good traits. However, I was rarely taught to touch base with myself, to consider what I wanted, or to appreciate my strengths, except when I made mistakes. Along the way I developed some negative opinions of myself. I often hid my authentic emotions, and often felt that I was not good enough. Most of my actions in my early years were done to seek approval and acceptance from people around me.

As I learnt about spiritual psychology, I realised how absolutely essential it is to be connected with that person within. The very first Hadith in Imam Al-Bukhari's hadith collections is about checking our intention behind every action we take.[90] All my actions were done for people's approval. I became very vulnerable to people's criticism. My self-worth was dependent on external sources outside of my control. In my early years of parenting, I was exhausted and unhappy. I was nice to other people but I could become overly strict and when I was under pressure, my children would cop my frustration.

Years later I learnt that to improve my state of well-being, I needed to like myself. I must do good from the right place within. Pleasing people was unpredictable and pointless. There will always be someone who disagrees or dislikes me. It was motivating to learn that doing good for goodness' sake would improve my holistic wellbeing. Understanding that the right intention and my best effort would ultimately boomerang back to me was powerful. I stopped living for people's praises.

If my self-discovery resonates with you, you may wonder as an adult: what can I do? The simple answer is, start with the part you want to change most. I would like to suggest the following questions to ask yourself:

1. What do I look like when I yell at my child?
2. What do I sound like when I am angry?
3. What was happening immediately before losing my temper?
4. Why am I behaving this way?

In your own time, I would like to propose for you to dig deep in order to become aware of the following: look beneath your emotion iceberg, and examine your narratives to raise your self-awareness.

Beneath Your Emotion Iceberg

The iceberg analogy is a widely used term to explore behaviour, motivation, success, writing style, and competency, to name a few. Its origin can be traced back to Freud's iceberg model of human behaviour. This model suggests that a visible problem or symptom is often connected to deeper issues beneath a person's conscious level.[91] What people see is only a tip of greater complexities underneath.

This analogy effectively offers a visual image to denote the necessity of looking deeper than what meets the eye.

What is observable is only the tip of the whole story. In the iceberg of success, for instance, what we see is the result, a moment of glamour or elation of triumph. Beneath it is a blend of events, circumstances, training, experiences, beliefs, perceptions and reasons that motivate the individual; not to mention the sacrifices, the tears and sweat, disappointments, the discipline and realistically, the multiple failures that led to the moment of victory.

There are two phases in which to manage your emotions: what to do on the spot, and what to do with your emotions after the immediate situation has passed.

Phase 1

As soon as you sense there is a surge of emotions in you, I recommend practising the following four steps:

- Acknowledge we are having an emotional moment
- Press the pause button
- Name it, and
- Examine the situation

Acknowledge. Just like when you see the steam coming out of the kettle you say, 'The kettle is boiling', you acknowledge what is happening without judgment. Sue Langley, CEO of the Langley Group, recommends people to treat emotions as 'data'. Next time you catch yourself in the middle of blowing your fuse, take a deep breath and tell yourself 'I have some data coming in.'[92] Acknowledging you are having an emotional moment is like grabbing hold of your child running in full speed towards a busy road by the arm. No more, no less.

Pause. Change your position. Have a sip of water. Take

a deep breath and sit down. Changing from standing to the sitting position lowers your blood pressure.

As a Muslim, it is our regular practice of supplications and remembrance of God that comes to our rescue. The last thing you need is to open the window to let the wind in that sets the fire into a raging inferno. As soon as you remember God, the demon stops egging you on. Recite supplications that give you relief. I find repeating 'Laa hawla wa laa quwwata illa billah' (There is no might or power except Allah) multiple times has a quick calming effect on me. If I sense I am getting angry or feeling scared or nervous, reciting several times Ayatul Kursi[93] or Surah al-Ikhlas[94] helps. Say it with conviction. Once you have calmed down, you are then in a better position to see the situation more objectively.

It only takes a few seconds to regain your composure, and you are now in a calmer position to manage yourself and the situation.

Name it. Take a good look at your emotional state and ask yourself: 'What is it that I am feeling here?' Is it sadness, anger, rage, disappointment, frustration, embarrassment…? Whatever it is, name it without judgment. Emotions are part and parcel of being human. There is nothing wrong with feeling those emotions. It is what you do with it that matters. Once you are able to name your emotion/s, you can work on gaining clarity of the issue at hand. It also automatically stops you from heading into an exchange with your child which you may regret later.

Examine. Is your child's behaviour something that warrants discipline, and if it is, what is the best approach you can think of, other than screaming, banging your pots or throwing your shoe at her?

By taking the four quick steps, you immediately prevent yourself from *reacting* to the situation. At the same time you have allowed yourself the psychological space to acknowledge your own emotions. You are then in a better position to *respond* to the situation.

You may decide that your child's behaviour deserves more understanding, more coaching or simply firmer discipline. Do so after you have had a chance to give it more thought. This way you can do the disciplining with all the right reasons minus the toxic fumes.

You may identify after the quick pause that you were bordering on overreacting. The four quick steps may just save you from exploding out of your emotion iceberg. Many times the child's behaviour is only a trigger. It may very well be the straw that broke the camel's back. Be careful not to dump the entire load of your emotions onto the child. By catching yourself in the moment, you could potentially have saved yourself from diving into a pit that you will feel regretful about later.

Phase 2

The second phase to managing your emotions is more about regaining balance and processing your thoughts after the immediate situation had passed.

Decompress. If you exercised restraint on the spot, well done for curbing your flood of emotions! Your real work is yet to come. This phase helps you reset your calmness. It involves using your cathartic strategies. You are likely to still feel perturbed after you held back from an explosion. Pull out one or more of your cathartic tools to help you regain level-headedness. You do not want to suppress what you are feeling. Allow yourself time to process what happened. Everyone deals with emotions differently. Have a good cry. Write. Scrub the bathroom. Pace the footpath. Punch a sandbag. Do something that channels your heightened energy into something constructive, that will calm you down without causing harm to anyone, including yourself. It helps to have a few strategies you can choose from in case one is not appropriate for the situation at that point in time.

The kindest thing I do for myself during such moments is to be alone for a while, usually accompanied by a good cry. A good cry always lets off the steam for me. If possible, I would speak to someone I trust. This always gives me new perspectives but that someone may not always be available. At times I am not ready to talk about it just yet. That is when I find journaling helpful. Journaling is similar to having a monologue but it is less alarming to onlookers. Journaling gives me time to process my thoughts. It draws out emotions deep within me and usually after a session of journaling, I find relief. It is helpful that I still speak to someone about it later; but journaling is something within my immediate reach. It also helps me articulate my emotions.

Look into your emotion iceberg. What will you find beneath your emotion iceberg? Do not be afraid to examine yourself. Ask yourself questions such as, why am I so affected by X? What was I doing immediately before this incident? Was there something already bothering me that I took it out on X? You will find a long list of things such as your physical health, your energy level, your beliefs, a passing remark from someone, your childhood memories, your experiences, your triumphs, your values, your perceptions, your goals, your fears, your insecurities, your unfulfilled ambitions, your duties, your upbringing, the way you want to be seen, etc. All these have some part to play in the way you react to things.

The tape incident. My son was around seven years old when one evening I heard something and raced out of the kitchen. I caught him recording the theme song of Power Rangers on the television with a big grin on his face. He accidentally dubbed over a tape I treasured a great deal. It was a copy of his and his sisters' voices I once recorded for my parents who were living in the US. The beast in me came out. I scolded him hard in front of his sisters. His face dropped.

I only realised much later that in that moment, my outburst got recorded onto the tape. I heard myself for the first time how mad I sounded. My children still laugh about it today. They memorised every word I said and imitated every pitch I used. My actions certainly left a lasting impression on my children! It was the first time I became aware of what I sounded like in anger. I am so glad they did not have access to a video camera back then!

Children make mistakes without necessarily intending to disobey their parents. They are forgetful and careless. In my experience, boys are more prone to forget and become careless than girls. I need to remember they are still learning.

Now I can think of a number of ways to address my son's action. I could have given him a different tape to keep and do what he liked with it. He knew to never play with our Qur'an tapes. I should have marked and put away tapes that were important to me to avoid accidents like this. To put things in perspective, it was only a small segment that was lost. So what was the big deal even if the entire tape was dubbed over? I could have asked my parents for the original to make another copy if I really wanted to. It was not like I had never lost any tapes being tangled up in the recorder before. Hindsight is a wonderful thing. I cannot take back what I did but hearing the tape gave me an opportunity to learn a valuable lesson.

This is the whole point of my self-disclosure. We need to bring out the bad and the ugly if we honestly wish to look inward, but do not forget to be kind to ourselves too.

Emotional exhaustion. I came across a parenting article[95] in which the author said something that gave me a lightbulb moment. He said that sometimes parents lose their temper with their children not necessarily because the children had done anything wrong, but because they (the parents) are emotionally exhausted.

I felt a sharp stab in my heart as I read that statement. I had done that to my children when they were little and I am sure I was not the last parent who did that. It is obvious that this author is speaking from authentic experiences as a parent. His words are full of empathy and at the same time ring alarm bells in parents. Too often parents are caught up in their own emotions on top of the daily grind of responsibilities that they are exhausted not only physically, mentally, but more so emotionally without being aware of it.

'Sometimes parents lose their temper with their children not necessarily because the children had done anything wrong, but because they are emotionally exhausted!'

This simple statement explains how I turned from a calm and reserved young lady to a screaming, angry and irrational creature! I was totally unaware that my emotions were driving my behaviour. I carried on without realising the need to take stock of what was going on inside me. Besides seeking my children's forgiveness, I want to bring this lesson to younger parents to start making the inward connection sooner.

Gain clarity. When I was able to look deeper into my emotion iceberg, as well as what was influencing my reaction in that moment, I began to gain clarity and sought alternatives to my response. Learning about our own emotion iceberg helps us understand our thinking patterns, draw strength from our past experiences and withhold judgment of other's behaviour, including our children's. It reduces the frequency of behaving reactively. It helps us seek first to understand ourselves, then to develop empathy for others. We learn that there is so much more beneath a person's behaviour. Look deeper than what is apparent. Allow room for what you cannot perceive, yet.

Emotion icebergs are not always negative. Empathy and compassion drive you to treat others with kindness. Anger drives you to stand for justice. Understanding your emotions does not mean you only focus on your 'negative' emotions. Keep looking and you will find the strengths within you.

Examine Your Narratives

Like it or not, we all grow up with certain scripts in our heads. Some scripts serve us well, others get in our way of progress. Our mindset guides our thinking, and our actions are a manifestation of our thoughts. Narratives are what we tell ourselves. Most of the time these narratives play in the background of which we are rarely aware. In Langer's words, we do things mindlessly. Ellen Langer is a professor of psychology at Harvard University who spent close to four decades of her career studying the illusion of control, motivation and mindfulness. In her book *Mindfulness* Langer opens a window that allows us to see our mindlessness for ourselves, and how deliberate mindful practices can rewire our brain to change the way we think, which can impact positively on our physiology and general wellbeing[96].

Mindless Narratives

Mindless narratives are stories you believe but are not necessarily true. What are some of the mindless narratives that are doing disservice to our own wellbeing? Some examples include: 'I am not good enough', 'I do not know enough', 'I am not talented like X therefore I can never be as successful', 'Without Y I am a failure' or 'My life is like this because of Z'. They are stories you tell yourself. Granted they could not have come from nowhere. They are messages you received as a child, inferences you made as you grew up, and experiences that you took to reinforce your beliefs. Your mind draws on these inputs and you learn to see and interpret things a certain way. As you grew up you did not know how to decipher which thoughts were factual, and which thoughts were fictional. Many live into their adulthood and still do not know the difference. But you can learn to differentiate these thoughts. You have to be brave enough to challenge them. Ask yourself questions such as 'Why not?', 'Where did I get this idea from?', 'Can't I at least give it a go?'. Think about the things you have achieved, the difficulties you have overcome, the people who had helped you. Let your focus shift to facts. Unless you challenge your fear or insecurities head-on, you will continue to entrap your consciousness in your own narratives.

Dig Deep

When I learnt about emotion iceberg and narratives, I did many rounds of digging into my inner self. The tape incident afforded me many details for introspection. It was dubbed over for a reason. It was not the easiest of exercises but the benefits were well worth the effort. It helped me grow as a person, as a wife and as a parent. Through challenging my narratives, I discovered deeper issues that I never would have realised otherwise.

What was beneath my anger when my son dubbed over the tape? The trigger was disobedience. Underneath the trigger, was the importance I placed on the children's precious voices I tried to preserve. What else? I was annoyed by the interruption while I was cooking. Once I allowed myself to dig deep, multiple issues came flooding out. I asked myself, what was going on with me at the time? I began to acknowledge that I was tired; no, I was exhausted. I had no one to turn for help. I was studying, working and volunteering in the community. My energy was often in deficit. Every morning from the time the alarm clock jolted me out of my deep sleep until I flopped my head on the pillow again some 16 hours later, I rarely had a moment to myself. I neglected my own needs. I lost touch with myself. My sense of self was slipping away.

I identified my low tolerance for imperfection during that period. I wanted perfection in everything I did, including how my children turned out.

What else was simmering inside? Under the guise for perfection, my narrative said I was not good enough because I failed my parents. I discovered that my decisions were affected by a need, subconscious yet strong, to please my parents. In fact, all I ever knew to do was striving for people's approval. The narrative in my head was that I disappointed my parents by getting married before I got my degree. I interpreted that as having failed their expectation of me.

What else did I learn about myself? I realised I was lonely. For long term economic stability of the family my husband chose to pursue his postgraduate studies. To make ends meet we both had to take up shift work on weekends, handing our children to each other as we would in a relay. I saw my exhausted husband an hour or so each day. We barely communicated. I felt unfulfilled, neglected.

Now I can see I was not studying for my own satisfaction. I drove myself to the ground to compensate for what I thought I failed to do. In that state of complete unawareness of the narrative I was operating from, I was convinced that the solution to my problems at that time was to go back to university. In hindsight I did it at the expense of my own wellbeing. I had no idea I was off balance. I lost a lot of weight. I became a control freak. I was impatient. My energy budget was in deficit and my mood was low. My studies were a band-aid over a rift of much deeper issues.

That was the real issue. After so many years I finally came face to face with my own demons.

What I needed most was for someone wise to show me another perspective of my situation, to remind me to practise gratitude, to connect with myself, and most of all, to practise self-compassion.

This is not a question of whether I loved my children. There was a reason for my crabbiness. I was not my *best self*. I suspect I suffered from undiagnosed mild depression for many years. I wonder how many parents out there are struggling to juggle the many demands on them while plagued by their unhelpful narratives? Back then what I really needed was to undo, to do less, and just be, in order to appreciate the blessings in my life. Instead, I overloaded and overstretched myself, for what? For that mindless narrative I held onto since I was child.

Moving Forward

Do I feel guilty over the repercussions of living by my narratives? Yes, I do, painfully so. The silver lining to this dark cloud is that it has motivated me to get acquainted with my inner self, in order to give my best self to my loved ones. It forced me to be honest with myself. It taught me to have empathy with myself. I feel energised when I see the potential to share my experience to help others.

To restore peace, I am working on getting past the guilt, and it is another ongoing process. This reminds me of a story my son shared with me of a Turkish wise man when he asked a question, 'If you ride the donkey facing backwards, who is navigating your journey?' We both laughed at this comical scene so much until tears ran out of my eyes. When I collected myself, I knew it was something I needed to hear. The past is there to either give you joy or help you grow. If it gives you pain, it is telling you to dig deeper so you can find the wound that needs to heal. The only time you look back is when you need to get yourself unstuck. Dwelling on past wounds stops you from moving forward. Masking over them will only make matters worse. The donkey may just carry you to more places that further complicate your life. If the wound is too much for you to deal with alone, seek professional help to guide you out of your emotional tangle.

Happiness is an aspect of wellbeing. Actively engaging in meaningful activities is a proven way to make you happy. Sonja Lyubomirsky's Happiness Pie[97] has provided me with uplifting information on *working for* happiness. Based on close to twenty years of research Lyubomirsky finds that 50% of people's happiness levels can be explained by genetically determined set points, such as genes, intelligence or chemical predisposition, 10% due to circumstances, and 40% from intentional activities. Quoting Benjamin Disraeli who said 'There is no happiness without action', Lyubomirsky posits that the 'fountain of happiness can be found in how you behave, what you think and what goals you set every day of your life.' This means that even for identical twins who have the same DNA make up with a low set point for happiness and the same upbringing, each child has 40% chance to work on intentional activities that will give them very different outcomes in life.[98]

Examining your inner self helps you see how you got to where you are. Empathy allows you to face what you have been carrying up until now. As you gain clarity about your narrative, you have a choice to either continue operating

Watering the Roots

from the same narrative, or challenge it and make intentional activities to change your way forward.

My parents had hopes and aspirations for me only because they believed in me. What had happened was in the past. I have accepted how those narratives came to be a part of me for many long years. Being able to figure out my mindless narratives was a giant step forward in my personal growth. I can choose to focus on the 40% of my intentional activities that are within my control to find meaning in what I do every day. It is never too late to remount my donkey so I can look forward to where I want to go for the rest of my journey.

Although it was a long process to connect inwardly, it was well worth the effort to see what was beneath my emotion icebergs and to understand some of my narratives. I recommend that you do the same. The earlier you attempt to understand your emotions and beliefs that do not serve you well, the sooner you gain clarity. Have the courage to face your own issues, if you have any. Although the process can be confronting, discovering the deeper issues facilitates growth. Making mistakes with your children is not synonymous to being a failure of a parent. Who does not make mistakes? The crux of the matter is your recognition of the need to grow as a parent. It has to start from yourself. Do not forget, you are a parenteer. You are continuously finding your way because you desire to stay on track to reach your destination.

The heartening thing to remember is that you *can* change your perspective. You can *choose* what to do with your narrative. *Free* yourself from whatever narrative that is not serving you in a positive way. Engage in intentional activities to be positive. It is never too late to start the process. As long as you see the value in this process God Almighty will unveil for you what you need to learn.

What serves one well to connect inwardly besides self-awareness, is self-care. This brings us to the second practice I would like to highlight to connect inwardly: self-care.

Self-Care

Apart from self-awareness, self-care is a major inward connection practice that few of us were taught to do. To benefit from the calm and cool headedness most parents need, the practice of self-care is a must.

We are always reminded at the beginning of each flight that in cases of emergency, we should put the oxygen mask on ourselves *before* we turn to help others. I love using this analogy for parents. Is this in line with Islamic teachings? God says 'O you who believe, save yourselves and your family from a fire whose fuel is human and stones…'.[99] God commands us to save ourselves first then our family. It makes every sense. You are in no position to save anyone if you are in need of being saved. Self-care is a duty not a choice when you have others in your care.

As a parent, you are the rock for your children. Your children's sense of security comes from the stability in you, both in form and spirit. You need to be well in order for your children to be well. Your wellbeing ripples onto your children; and how well you care for yourself sets the scene for how well they learn to care for themselves.

Self-care is a huge topic on its own. I have selected two areas to focus on: physical care and self-preservation.

Physical Care

Healthy living is a popular topic to which people have paid attention for generations. A healthy lifestyle is indeed a worthwhile pursuit. The body is our vehicle that accompanies us through our worldly journey. Good health affords us the ability to function, worship, work, rest and play well. Putting in the right fuel and regular maintenance allows for optimum performance in life. Information abounds on the importance of nutrition, exercise, recreation and sleep for our wellbeing.

The only thing I wish to highlight in this regard is how astoundingly pro-health are the prescribed and recommended Islamic practices. All things permissible are good for us and all things prohibited are detrimental to our wellbeing. I met a Burmese young man who told me that what attracted him to Islam was the rituals of cleansing (Wudu) before the five daily prayers. The COVID-19 pandemic that swept the globe in 2020 is a sobering reminder of just how pro-wellbeing Islam is. In our ritual cleansing, we wash our hands, face and feet, we rinse our nose, gargle water five times more than others who do not observe this ritual. How many more aspects of our health and wellbeing have we been blessed from this lifestyle of submission to our Creator? To mention a few, eating halal food, performing the formal prayers, observing the annual fasting etc., are all examples that benefit our holistic wellbeing—the social, mental, spiritual and the physical dimensions.

Your adherence to a healthy lifestyle is the model your children are likely to adopt. Next let us look at wellbeing practices of self-preservation.

Self-preservation

Islam is the middle path. It is in tune with a person's nature. It promotes moderation and balance. Self-preservation is something I believe every parent need to learn and implement.

Over-worked, over-stressed, and overwhelmed parents are often depleted in energy and patience, two among the most important resources in parenting. Ask yourself: when are you most likely to get angry and frustrated? In my case back in the day, it was always in the morning when I was pressed for time to get everyone to school on time (hence wanting for patience) and in the evening when I was low on energy but still needed to soldier on. Next, we look at energy budget and practise being kind to yourself.

Energy Budget

All those who drive know how important it is to keep track of the fuel gauge at the start and throughout the journey. We gauge our fuel according to the trip we are about to take. If we find our tank low but we need to travel a long distance, the first thing we do is to fill up the fuel tank.

Parental responsibilities never end. As the number of responsibilities increases, so do the demands on our energy. Energy is what keeps us going. Yet we rarely pay attention to it until we become severely depleted.

I once did an assignment called the Mood Meter for a course in Positive Psychology and Wellbeing. I had to track my mood every two hours and choose a descriptive word to place on a tracking graph. For each entry I jotted down brief notes on what I was doing around that time. I had to do this every day for two consecutive weeks. At the end of the exercise, I saw patterns of my mood changes. I observed what activities/situations usually lifted my mood and what tended to affect my mood negatively. This was what I discovered about what affected my mood: sleep and my children's wellbeing had major effects on me. I also identified what I could do to increase the likelihood of staying in a good mood most of the time.

Adopting the concept of Mood Meter, I wish to suggest that overworked parents do an exercise tracking your Energy Budget. Record your own energy level as you take on one task after another in a day.

Our energy budget for each day is different, not unlike the budget allocated to each public sector by the government from one year to the next. To give you a visual, let us imagine our energy level is like the power bars on our mobile phones. If we were unwell, or did not have enough sleep, our energy bars that day would be less to start with. Imagine that we start our day with full 10 bars of energy after a good night's sleep. For each task we take on, we evaluate how we feel during and after that task. These tasks may be physical, emotional or mental. Demands on energy have no shape unless we learn to pay attention to them. Sometimes we feel tired for no apparent reason. It could be something on our mind that is consuming our energy at a cellular level.

Some clues to assess if you are experiencing a drop in your energy include:

- Do you detect your mood going flat?
- Are you finding it difficult to stay focused?
- Are you rushing to finish your chores?

- Do you feel a little impatient with people (more likely with your children and your spouse)?
- Do you feel slightly anxious about the tasks ahead of you?

Once you become aware of the importance of gauging your activities according to your energy level, you learn to do three things: recharge your energy, conserve your energy, and plug your energy drainers.

Recharge. If you have school aged children, it is probably a wise thing for you to replenish your energy after the rush hour in the morning. Spending some alone time to meditate, exercise, work on your hobby, water the garden, listen to an audio book, or just savour a cup of tea without anyone interrupting are some ideas you might want to consider before you dive into your next pressing chore. For a busy parent, taking a Sunnah nap at mid-day is highly recommended yet such a luxury.

A number of warning signs when my energy budget is very low include feeling overwhelmed by all the things on my mind. I start doubting my ability to complete all there is to be done. Sometimes I feel like I need a good cry for no reason. Pay attention to what your body tells you as well. I get a dull ache in my lower back, or the more severe sign is a pounding headache.

When I detect any of these warning signs, I force myself to stop thinking and I close my eyes for a few minutes. If possible, lie down for 15 minutes, or 30 minutes, however long you can afford. Set the alarm so you will not be late to pick up the children from school, for example. If I was in the car, I would do a few rounds of 'dhikr' (remembrance of God) along with some deep breathing exercise while I waited at the school gate. I sometimes forget to eat. Grabbing something nourishing can quickly give my energy a well needed boost. Past experiences tell me that after a power nap, things always look brighter and feel more achievable. If you have younger children, try to lie down while they take their nap.

If we check our energy budget often enough, we will have some idea when we need a quick top up somewhere along the way.

Energy conservation. There are always so many things you need to prioritise. Do not forget that your wellbeing is one of those priorities too. I tend to organise my to-do list the night before. Not taking on too much when the demands are already high is a reasonable approach to conserving our energy. Conserving energy is like putting the brakes on what we do. Slow down and remember to breathe.

Conserving your energy is also a safety measure, for you and your children. You reduce the chances of sliding into deficit. We have all experienced times when we feel we no longer have the energy to lift another finger yet a child's sudden alarming screams can make us jump to her rescue. Reserves are to be used for such rainy days. Try not to dip into your reserves too often. Most things can wait if you allow them; the dishes in the sink, for example. They will not run away, I promise. It will be a breeze to get through them after you have had a break.

Be mindful that conserving your energy means you have to say 'no' to certain things. Young parents, especially young mothers, need to develop this awareness and find ways to conserve your energy. The responsibility of raising children does not become lighter as the children grow older. You may not be as physically exhausted, but your teenage children will surely stress you mentally. New challenges will keep you on your toes.

I no longer have young children to take care of yet I am still learning to get this one right. I guess one never ceases to learn and grow, even with things you thought you knew well already.

One of my trips home from visiting my husband in Saudi was a typical example of me forgetting to conserve my energy. After the long flight I continued to observe the final days of the month-long fast in Ramadan. I was home for two months. Thinking I had only limited time at home I said 'yes' to practically everything that needed doing plus whatever else that popped up. First, I got talked into holding an Eid party (one of the Muslim celebrations) straight after Ramadan for 30 people. We had the floor renovation lined up immediately after Eid and I added painting the interior walls of the house to the list. I had to deal with a sea of stuff that spilled out from the bookshelves and cupboards following the flooring installation. In the midst of all these I flew interstate to attend a wedding and went on a trip to Malaysia with my daughter. As if that was not enough, several things broke down days before I was due to fly back to Saudi. This meant calling the water corporation, the plumber and the reticulation repairer. Thankfully, as exhausted as I was, I did not lose my temper with anyone. I took little breaks when I felt I needed one. However, I took a huge withdrawal from my energy reserve.

I could not remember how I made my way to Saudi. All I remembered was a desperate need to sleep. I would fall asleep on the couch five nights out of seven shortly after our early dinner around 5pm in the middle of a conversation with my husband. I could not wait to pray Salatul Isha (night prayer) so I could crawl into bed. I did the bare minimum during the day. For several weeks I felt like a ragdoll. My over optimism with my energy budget left me in deficit for weeks that followed. I promised myself I would be mindful to conserve my energy in future and not overstretch myself again.

Detect and plug energy drainers. We have all done the mathematics problem at school calculating the time it takes to fill up a tank from a tap running at one rate with a hole that is leaking at a slower rate. I never liked that problem. I used to think, why doesn't someone just block the hole to let the tank fill up?

Recognising and managing energy drainers is like plugging a hole as soon as you detect a leak. Plugging our energy drainers is not only recommended; it is necessary.

Here is a demonstration of how a person plugs an energy drainer. A few years ago a friend of mine and I attended a public lecture at a university. When we came out of the lecture room, time for Salatul Maghrib (prayer right after sunset) came in. I suggested to my friend to pray on campus before we went home since the prayer room was on our way to the car park. To my surprise my friend hurriedly excused herself. She could not even wait to walk over with me. The next day she called to apologise for her behaviour. She said she felt uneasy from being in the lecture room and she followed her instinct. She called it one of her energy drainers. I have always known this dear friend to be intuitive. She is one of very few wise people I have met who are very attentive to their inner state of balance.

She can detect any slight imbalance in energy and she will respond accordingly, be it a situation, a space or a person. It really is a privilege to watch and learn from this amazing woman who has been through some very tough trials in life and still came out calm, composed and gracious.

How to detect energy drainers? By listening to our inner voice. We have all seen young children withdraw from certain people, or resist stepping into a place. Their senses can be sharper than most adults because they follow their intuition. What we need to respect is that internal sensor which we may have ignored or suppressed for too long. Learn to get acquainted with your innate balancer again. Your inner voice may appear in a flash. Sometimes it is an energy shift. Occasionally you detect physical discomfort, like what my friend felt that evening. Watch your own breathing patterns and physical reactions.

Notice when you feel uneasy, or your energy suddenly feels flat, or you sense the need to leave, the urge to go home, or just a need to step outside for some air. Pay attention and take a decisive action to stop the leakage. It is always helpful to prepare what to say or do for a quick exit from the scene when necessary. This is self-care most of us have not been taught.

Next, we explore self-preservation through being kind to ourselves.

Be Kind to Yourself

Christopher Germer, author of *The Mindful Path to Self-Compassion* suggests, 'A moment of self-compassion can save your day. A string of such moments can change the course of your life.'[100] Dr. Kristin Neff writes on her website, 'With self-compassion, we give ourselves the same kindness and care we'd give to a good friend.'[101] Being kind to yourself means to embrace yourself as you are, accepting not only what you do right and well, but also when you make mistakes, are hurt or sad. This does not mean you find excuses for your mistakes. Rather, treat yourself with kindness and understanding during such times until you regain your strength to move on.[102]

Self-compassion in itself is a field that has attracted much interest after Kristin Neff first took it to study at an academic level. It has since developed into a specialty in its own right within the field of Positive Psychology. I have included three points for discussion that contribute to being kind to yourself: be fair to yourself, forgive yourself, and speak to yourself like you would a close friend.

Be Fair to Yourself

How often are we paralysed by the fear of not doing a good job in raising our children? How many times are we pushing ourselves mercilessly to keep up our image or family reputation? Isn't it time that we do what is right for us and give ourselves a fair go?

Many times during the course of writing this book I wanted to throw the towel in because I passed unkind judgment on myself. Whenever my mind drew a blank, I heard this voice telling me, 'perhaps you are just not good enough to do it!' I compared myself with successful authors and experienced academics. In my mind I felt unless I produced something as fantastic my work is not worthy.

To my rescue one day my daughter sent me a link to an interview by Marie Forleo with author Elizabeth

Gilbert.[103] I felt like Elizabeth was directly speaking to me. She talked about dropping unrealistic expectations and getting on with completing what one set out to do. It was never about producing the most wonderful piece of work. It was only about getting the work done. Elizabeth advised her audience to stop the self-sabotage. We give our best at the time of doing, but how people see it is not our issue. That was exactly what I needed to hear! Parenting was no different. Parenting was never about raising the most perfect child.

In my early years of parenting, I let fear direct my decisions. I let the anxiety of how people would judge my parenting steer the way I raised my children. Truth is, those people did not exist. It was my fear that clouded my good sense. What I needed was to give myself permission to not be perfect. After freeing myself from people's judgment, I felt lighter, and my mind became clearer, and most amazingly, I began to slowly trust my instinct and to exercise wisdom, for what I considered right for my children.

There was an incident when I saw my children seized by fear and I knew, just as I needed to give myself a fair go, I needed to teach my children to give themselves a fair go.

That year two of my children were sitting for their Tertiary Entrance Examination. One afternoon I picked them up from school and they conversed with each other in the car. They shared with each other how they had no confidence whatsoever in the Calculus exam coming up. That was their final subject. They both said perhaps they would not bother going at all. A part of me was panicking for them. However, in that moment, I recognised how fear had taken hold of them. I told myself to separate their decision from my parenting. I bit my tongue and prayed for an opportunity to speak. They went on until we pulled up into our driveway. Suddenly one of them turned to ask me, 'Mum, what do you think?' Relieved at being invited to put my two cents in, I said, 'You are both old enough to make your own decisions. I am not going to tell you what to do. I can hear you are both worried you won't do well in this subject. Now that you've asked for my opinion, I would say, if I were you, I would turn up and just put my name down on the paper. Look through the paper, answer what I can, I have nothing to lose. I am confident you both know something. Put down what you know and leave the rest in the hands of God.'

Two days later, both of them turned up for their exam. When TEE results came out, Calculus was one of the four subjects that gave them a good aggregate for entry to their university courses.

Forgive Yourself

We have all made not-so-wise choices for our children at some stage. We have all lost our temper at them. Some of us look back wondering if we had been too soft, too hard, or not given them enough discipline, encouragement…

Be fair and forgive yourself. How many of us are plagued by guilt for certain things we regret we did or did not do in the past? This guilt becomes worse if we attribute our action to what is not going right for our children later in their lives.

While it is true that parents have a big part to play in our children's wellbeing; what we need to also keep in mind is that children, like us, are dynamic and resilient beings. We do what we humanly can. Our Creator has a plan for each of His creations. Not even parents are privy to foresee how each child will turn out. We must not forget that whatever happens, happens only by the will of our Creator.

To forgive our mistakes is to accept our human-ness. This does not mean we shrug off responsibilities for the mistakes we made. Admitting to our own mistakes is hard. Dwelling on them serves no one. The ultimate goal of well-being is attaining a tranquil heart. To apologise is within our control, so too is our efforts to amend our mistakes. We do what needs to be done to achieve peace in our own soul.

Fortunately, our Creator has shown us multiple ways to address our mistakes. We seek forgiveness from our Creator first and foremost. We ask for Guidance and strive to find better ways to do better. We can ask for our children's forgiveness if our children are old enough to understand. For as long as we are able to breathe and communicate, we can make amends with our children. We can learn, we can change, and we can do better.

Speak to Yourself Like You Would a Close Friend

If you are not used to speaking kindly to yourself, it is time you did. Kristin Neff points out that most people are very good at being kind to others, but harsh to themselves. This means that the majority of us have the skills and resources to be compassionate. We just need to include ourselves in that big circle of humanity to receive compassion, from ourselves.[104]

If you are like me, in the habit of beating yourself up over your human-ness, you need to practise playing the role of a good friend to yourself. Listen to the words you use when you criticise yourself. What would you say to a friend when you find her spiralling into self-criticism, self-doubt, self-loathing, and self-sabotage? You would first listen with empathy. You would remind her of her strengths. You would speak to her with kindness. Look beneath the surface and embrace the soul and spirit of this person called 'I'. Accept who 'I' am without judgment. Say to yourself, 'I am another human being just like anyone else.' 'I am feeling this way because I too experience pain, and suffering, just like everyone else.' Give yourself empathy and space to heal. It is just like tending a wound: be gentle, whether the wound is on someone else or on yourself. The last thing you want to do is to pour acid on it or to cut it deeper.

Neff makes the link between self-compassion and improved mental health and wellbeing. She speaks about three core components to self-compassion through her research.[105] These are: treating oneself with kindness; common humanity; and mindfulness.

Treating yourself with kindness is to give yourself the same compassion you would a friend, such as empathy, understanding, gentleness, encouragement. Common humanity is realising that suffering and pain are all part of being human. We are born imperfect. Do not isolate yourself from the rest of humanity. Mindfulness means to be in the moment. No judgment. You can only give yourself compassion if you are aware of your suffering. Once you do that, you will soon be able to move into a space of gratitude and open to possibilities.

Conclusion

Schools since the industrial revolution have largely become factories that produce graduates whose successes are defined by numbers. For those who have achieved pre-determined scores for 'success', they get to stay on the conveyor belt for further competition. Along the way many are 'eliminated', or left to stay on the margins of the conveyor belt, without providing them with the adequate support, guidance and direction they need in life.

Few schools help children to develop their creativity, or teach children how to live well. In recent times some elite private schools have invested in positive education through a whole school approach to build wellbeing and positivity into their curriculum. Not everyone has access to such privilege.

Parents, you are your child's first school. You play a key role in teaching your children to value who they are and to take good care of themselves. You also have the prime opportunity in your hands to mould their character from day one. Moral character is a dynamic process, not a static trait. Your examples and influence will form the basic building blocks of your children's values system. But first, practise inward connection yourself, then what is fundamentally valuable to you will ripple onto your children.

CHAPTER SEVEN
Vertical Connection

Knowing one's heart leads one to knowing himself, and the one who knows himself knows his Lord.[106]

WE ARE INHERENTLY dependent. We cannot afford to live without guidance. This chapter focuses on our inherent need to seek guidance from the Divine.

The moment we depend on our own intelligence and desires to lead our life is the moment we head toward confusion and chaos. Mankind never witnessed the magic of what a digital world can do for our lives like we are experiencing at present. Along with the unprecedented access to information and unimaginable conveniences in life is the looming destruction of the earth. If science and human intelligence were the ultimate tools for progress, can science and human intelligence really reverse the damage that is done?

The reality is, our life has an end, we are mortal beings, and our capabilities can only take us so far. We need to acknowledge our limitations. Our intellect has limitations. Our inner self has its good and bad tendencies. The most we can achieve is to use whatever resources available, to understand the world around us, to study the phenomena and things around us. New understandings and perspectives will continue to be uncovered. No one can claim absolute authority over knowledge. This is where we need our Creator.

This is where we need to admit that we need guidance. If we pay attention, guidance is plainly available to everybody. The heart (of knowing, not the physical organ) where the soul resides is the responsive centre built in us to receive our Creator's divine guidance. All we have to do is make a conscious effort to connect; this connection is what I call the Vertical Connection. Even angels say: 'We have knowledge only of what You [God] have taught us.'[107]

This realisation is shared by those who have faith in the Creator of all that exists. They all have one thing in common, that is submission to this higher being. They recognise there is more to life than the flesh and blood. There is something within human beings that gives them their unique existence. What makes them alive? Who keeps them alive? Who determines how long they live? Even with such advancement in medical and scientific interventions, doctors cannot give their patients life and they cannot compare human interventions to the body's self-healing abilities. Take sleep, for instance. The quality of drug-induced sleep cannot compare with a natural good night's sleep in terms of restfulness and restoration to a person's health.

Seek Guidance

The first thing we look for when unpacking a new appliance is its instruction manual. Mankind's life instruction manual is in God's revelations. He has continued to give mankind His instruction manuals through His divine revelations in the form of Holy Scriptures. By using God's revelations, which I consider as our 'road map', we can hope to find our way home. Not only that, throughout history of mankind, God has continuously sent a chain of His appointed prophets to give us life demonstrations to guide us.

Everything on this earth will perish. All that exists is absolutely dependent and imperfect. Everything dependent needs someone to depend on. We all want an emergency hotline that is available 24/7. In our time of need the slightest delay in response causes us anxiety and grief. Everything imperfect can only exist with the support of One who is perfect, who is strong and never fails to respond to calls of help, by His perfect timing.

Recognising and acknowledging there is a Creator is the first step. It is by design that humans innately have a need to worship a being greater than themselves. In order to fulfill this need, some have mistaken creations as their object of worship, such as a piece of wood, stone, people or even spirits, all of whom are creations, imperfect and dependent. They direct their worship to someone/something who is either inanimate nor capable of saving their own existence. This is the danger of following someone who uses their mind or imagination without divine guidance, particularly in matters of the soul. It is like taking a medicine concocted by someone who has no idea of what he is doing; and is himself in need of help. It is frightening to think that I once almost slipped into that hole of childish imagination of who God was. I will share this story with you a little later.

Our spiritual need is to be addressed only by the one who created our spirits. Likewise, to address our physical, emotional and intellectual needs, we need to seek knowledge from the one who created these faculties.

We discussed earlier in Chapter Five regarding a one-stop shop where all our needs can be met by a centralised authority. It is not only Muslims who have access to this authority. This same central message runs through all the scriptures of the Abrahamic faith. Mankind believed in monotheism since the beginning of its creation. It was since the time of Prophet Noah (peace be upon him) that people began to set up idols instead of worshipping God. Throughout history the chain of prophets and messengers of God have ALL been charged to convey the same message to mankind: to worship the One and Only God, who has no partner, who begets not and is not begotten.

Let us fast forward to the seventh century Arabian Peninsula. In the pre-Islamic era Arabs believed in God in their traditions, except that they had confusing ideas regarding the perfect nature of God. Their worshipping multiple idols implied imperfections and inadequacies in the almighty attribute of God. Although they did acknowledge that no one could send down rain from the sky except God; and, they knew that the sun, the moon and the stars could not have existed by their own will, nor could these heavenly bodies rise and set without the permission and might of God; yet they followed their forefathers in worshipping 360 gods, and each was believed to have power in a different matter. Thus, they projected human limitations onto God. A true God worthy of our devotion and obedience is one who is capable of all things, who does not need any deputies to help Him guard all affairs of His creations.

During his twenty-three-year mission to convey God's message to mankind, Prophet Muhammad (peace and blessings be upon him) spent thirteen years re-connecting the souls of his people to the One God. His key message is none other than recognising and submitting to the One who is the reason that all exists. I mention this historical fact to highlight the continuity of the same message through human history. The teaching objective of Prophet Muhammad (peace and blessings be upon him) was none other than inviting people to return to God. My question is: What should you bear in mind when introducing the Creator to your child? The following are a few pointers for you to consider.

Spirituality Before Rituality

Marwan Chaar of Raindrop Academy observes a common flaw in religious education around the Muslim world that

> ... the focus is on the procedural instead of the core of what Islam has to offer: purification of the heart.... They are being overwhelmed with the mundane and forget the fundamental point:

sacred knowledge should bring you closer to God.[108]

Growing up in a Muslim family made my practices such as fasting and adhering to a Halal diet easy. The phrase 'haram' (impermissible) used by my elders from memory gave me a sense that there is an authority, so great that even my parents and grandparents had to obey. Even then I lived in ignorance for years about my Creator.

My concept of God was seriously murky. I always saw my grandmother praying on a maroon-coloured prayer mat in the direction of a closed wardrobe door in the small bedroom we shared. Being the private person she was, it was only on rare occasions I got a peek at what was inside the wardrobe. It was during one of those rare moments when I spotted a framed black and white photo from a distance and in my little head I linked that image to God. I thought that was why Grandma prayed in that direction.

It was not until many years later I learnt that no human eye could ever perceive God. God tells us in the Qur'an, 'No vision can take Him in, but He takes in all vision; and He is the Subtle, the Aware.'[109] I had to consciously dissociate this image from God in my head!!! May Allah forgive me!

As I learnt more about my religion, I gradually pieced these snippets of memory together. Grandma prayed in that direction because it was where it pointed to the Ka'bah—the focal point in Makkah towards which all Muslims around the world prayed. She kept the wardrobe door closed to make sure there were no images in front of her. I found out much later that the image in that frame was one of my cousins standing on the bough of a tall tree looking down.

This was a secret I kept to myself. I was too ashamed to tell anyone about this until now. My sharing of this secret now is not to put blame on anyone, including myself. In fact, I have nothing but gratitude for the elders in my life for having helped me to form my identity as a Muslim the best they knew how. Even though I started with murky concepts about my Lord, He the Most Forgiving and Most Merciful never abandoned me. This immense gratitude has motivated me to share my thoughts here with other adults who have Muslim children in their care.

What motivated me to share this story here is the realisation of what critical information adults should bear in mind when introducing God to their children. We adults sometimes take things for granted. From a child's viewpoint, however, there is very little information upon which they can draw to help them relate to new information. In developmental psychology, young children first learn from concrete, tangible things of which their senses can perceive: hence questions such as 'where is God?', 'what does God look like?' or 'how come I cannot see God?' are common. I hear the teacher in me screaming: 'We need to spell things out clearly and simply from the start!' Here are two quick pointers to share with parents:

1. Tell the child about the concept of one God and His attributes. The one concept about God we must not leave out is that we are not able to see Him in this life! Whatever images we have of Him, He is greater, and He is the Creator of them all.
2. Teach the child to adopt the Two-Fold practice.

Point to all the signs that show God exists. Develop the habit of looking beyond what their senses can perceive and relate everything back to the Creator.

Thankfully young children are very spiritual and have great imagination. Their minds are clear and not yet bound by logic. This is actually a prime time for them to learn about God, not rituals, not rules, but the greatness, the might, the mercy, the love, the compassion and the all-seeing, all-hearing, most forgiving attributes of God.

Help Young Children Connect

Once I attended a talk my husband gave at a community where he used a story to explain the first part of a Muslim's proclamation of faith: 'I bear witness that there is *no deity* except God'. He emphasised how the proclamation started with a negation— 'no deity except...'. He then told a story to highlight the importance of starting with a negation. The story goes that there once was a guitar instructor. Two students went to learn from this acclaimed guitar instructor. The first student could play a little while the second did not know how to play at all. The instructor said he would charge the first student double what he would the second. Puzzled, the first student asked for an explanation. The instructor replied, 'I need to undo all the wrong techniques and bad habits you have picked up before I can start with you on my instructions. Whereas with your friend, I can start with him on a clean slate straight away!'

That teacher's rationale rings true to my experience of that image I had about God in my head! The ground needs to be cleared before any seed is sown. An artist's great work begins on a clean canvas. A Muslim's proclamation begins with a negation—no deities except the One God. Whatever images we could form about God, are all from creations of what our senses could perceive. Our imagination is limited to only what we perceive. That is why we need to negate before we affirm. We need to clearly understand that 'There is nothing that resembles Him' and 'Vision perceives Him not; but He perceives all vision'. To know God one needs to purge all attributions of the created to receive descriptions of God given by God Himself! In my case, it was not what my parents and grandparents said or did that caused my confusion. The problem lay in what was not said. I had no dots to connect to start with, so somehow I made do with what my small mind could conjure up to make sense of things. The mind clearly needs guidance!

Therefore, Muslim parents have a duty to select the appropriate dots and help their children connect them to know God. The following are suggestions parents may take on board:

- Read them stories about God's power, attributes, infinite knowledge and wisdom
- Expose them to the amazing nature, to animals, and let them observe the signs that point to the presence of God
- Encourage children to ask questions. There is no such thing as a wrong question. It is their right to know. In Chinese language the term for seeking knowledge is called 'Xue Wen', which directly translates into 'Learning through Asking'

Point them to the beauty of His creations, the varieties

of living species and the mercy and love between parents and their young in the animal kingdom etc. All of these and much more are created by God. Let them feel their heartbeats and pulse; the air that flows in and out of their nostrils; let them thank God for their ability to walk, run and hold objects with their hands. The dots are everywhere. You can pick any to help them join the dots to make the vertical connection.

No Connection, No Faith

Many Muslim parents consider it a crisis that their children are questioning their faith. In regards to this issue, there are many factors involved. This is a huge topic that should be discussed in-depth among Muslim scholars, educators and parents. I only wish to share a few thoughts from personal experiences.

Scare Tactic For Conformity

I have spoken to many Muslims who recall being coerced into conformity with religion through fear. This approach is not unique among Muslim communities. One of the weapons adults use to make children conform is using punishment of hellfire more than the mercy and love of God to gain compliance.

The following encounter is an example of how children are made to behave in mosques.

My son visited different cities and sometimes he would stay in local mosques wherever he travelled. Someone once asked him out of concern if he ever felt scared. We were puzzled by her question. She explained that as a child she was warned about running around or making noise in the mosque because there were Jinns (a creation of God that operates in a different frequency of which human eyes cannot see) in the mosque. What a way to make children behave!

I also suspect the style of parenting and teaching in greater part of the last century where children ought to be seen and not heard may have provided the perfect ground for this approach to be considered as an effective approach. It gives adults the satisfaction in attaining immediate conformity from young children.

Cart Before The Horse

Some teachers and parents, though well intended, taught Islam to their children with the same approach their parents and teachers had taken to teach them: back to front. The focus was more on practice than spiritual connection. The teaching tends to focus on rules and rituals.

It takes much effort and creativity to help children connect spiritually, whereas rules and rituals are observable, quantifiable and measurable, and therefore easier to demonstrate, to assess and to put down a grade to indicate progress. Spiritual connection is intangible.

I have a thought to share. Rules and regulations are there to set the boundaries for the believers. For a person who has no idea who God is, rules and regulations are the mere mechanics that provide a person its operative structure. Rules and rituals offer a person the visible discipline and shape of what a believer should do and looks like, but the inner spirit remains disconnected. Many may grow up to find the connection but many lose interest. This back to front approach is hit and miss.

What happens when children begin to shift from passive, rote learning to active inquiry and critical thinking? Parents and teachers are lost when their children are no longer content with the *what* and *how* to dos, and they begin to ask the *whys, why nots, what fors* and *what's in it for mes*.

We have been given our special endowments of soul, free will and intellect for a reason. In my humble opinion, this approach of introducing the dos and don'ts before the whys and to whom we do it for needs urgent review. The rules and regulations may harness the body and limbs, but the soul and the mind need to be properly connected first. What is the use of having a kitchen full of appliances when the electricity supply has not even been connected?

I do not have all the answers. Application in real life situations is the most effective form of connection. One area of research you may want to look into is Values or Character Education. I have chosen an example to share below.

Values Education

Tim Sharp (aka Dr. Happy), in one of his weekly newsletters wrote, 'Why do good people do bad things?'[110] He described a scenario in which a generally good person happened to do something that 'failed himself and those who were relying on him. He's led himself and them down. And everyone involved was disappointed, frustrated and even a little angry.'[111] Dr. Happy explained that everyone could sometimes be influenced by external factors to make a wrong decision. The person is always responsible for the decision he made. The strategy he underscored in that discussion was to know our values, to have clarity and to use our values to guide us in our decision making.

Values include moral ethics, rules of conduct, standard of behaviour, to mention a few. These are core principles a person or society holds dear for guidance. Values vary from people to people, from society to society. There are certain values that are timeless and common across cultures and societies. These are universal values accepted by all. One can almost guarantee that values such as honesty, justice, integrity, kindness and responsibility are included in most forms of values education. People who live by any of these values are considered to have goodness in them.

Given the diversity of cultures and values, have you ever wondered how these universal values came about that never wavered from their position throughout humanity? Is it any coincidence that they happen to sit so right with humanity?

To a believer, the answer is crystal clear. God created us and placed in us an internal compass to know and appreciate these values. The unity of authority on this, on us, and every natural system in the universe came from the one source. This one source is none other than the Almighty God who desires for us to choose what is right and good to our own benefit. I have taken a few examples of what is built in us for discussion.

Love

How do we love someone? We need first to get to know him. We gather information about him. We watch and observe what we experience to test if they match. To get to know our Creator, we observe and reflect on His Greatness. We learn His beautiful names and attributes. Among all those attributes, Al-Wadood (The most loving) is a good one to start with. Vertical Connection starts with love.

Volumes have been written on love. People write songs and poems about love, die for love and make billions of dollars out of love. Bear in mind that all the love in this world, in its sum total adds up to 1% of the love of Al-Wadood. All forms of love originate from the source, Al-Wadood. It is an emotion the Creator instilled in every one of us. A child learns to love by receiving love. The primary caregiver in a child's early days play a key role in making the child feel safe, secure and cared for. The primary caregiver is the bridge to the child getting to know Al-Wadood. The capacity and extent of Al-Wadood is immeasurable.

Is love a verb or a noun? Covey says love is a verb, it 'is a value that is actualized through loving actions.'[112] He says one manifests one's love through doing nice things for their loved ones. This is true. I prefer the word 'serving' than 'doing nice things'. The word serving has added layers of meaning such as humility, responsibility, and a rewarding act. A responsible man would work his hands to the bones to provide for his family. A mother would jump to her baby's cry from the depth of her slumber. The companions would trade in their lives to protect the life of their beloved Prophet Muhammad (peace and blessings be upon him). These are various manifestations of love.

A few years ago a true story of a ten-year-old girl was featured on China Liaoning official television channel. Bin-Ling (known as Binbin) had a conflict with her father.

She told the audience that her father wanted to find a family to adopt her but she flatly refused. The man whom she addressed as her father was not related to her. The story took the audience back to a decade earlier when she was found abandoned in a carton, barely two months old. He took pity on the baby and took her home to raise her. For her happiness and wellbeing this man never got married. When Binbin barely started school her father had an accident at work and lost his sight. She rose up to the challenge and shouldered all the responsibilities about which children her age have not the faintest clue. After school, Binbin spent all her time at home cooking, cleaning, washing and doing her schoolwork as well as looking after her disabled father.[113]

What gave Binbin the strength to persevere with such heavy responsibilities at such a tender age? It was love. How did she know she was loved? Through her father's caring service. She received love and she learnt to give love. She appealed to the television audience to help her out because her father was diagnosed with end term gall bladder cancer. The father explained that the sensible thing for him to do upon learning his condition was to search for a good family to take care of Binbin. This became a conflict between them because all Binbin wished for was to stay and take care of her father till the end. Her story moved tens of thousands of viewers in China. Some generously donated to help keep them together for as long as possible.

From this true story, I understand love both as a verb and a noun; it is also an emotion. Action and emotion are intertwined. One triggers and extends to the other. I am talking about the kind of love which is given without expectations, that is unconditional. For the Prophet says:

'None of you truly believes until he wishes for his brother what he wishes for himself.'[114]

It was out of sympathy and mercy that the man took on the task of a parent to raise that abandoned baby a decade ago. The emotion became the energy and purpose for his action. His actions were received, interpreted and internalised by the child as love. This became the energy and reason that propelled her to take on all the work when the father lost his sight. The recent diagnosis had dealt another heavy blow to both of their lives. It was again out of love that the father attempted to make suitable arrangements for the child's future; in the same token, it was the child's love that drove her to appeal for help on China's national television because she said, 'if I went to another family, who will take care of my father?' There was not a dry eye in the live audience. Again, it was love that motivated total strangers to assist this man and his daughter.

Love is something most parents naturally demonstrate from the time a child is conceived, right through till the end of his life. From early on, parents' provision of care, comfort, security, consoling, fulfilling of promises, being there for the child emotionally and physically, are all built into the wonderful mosaic of a child's emotional wellbeing. Parents from certain cultures, mine included, tend to express love only through their actions, but seldom vocalise it. I urge parents to exercise the Two-Fold, Double-Selection principle. Parents should go the extra mile to trace these emotions and actions as all originated from Al-Wadood. In order for them to help their children make the vertical connection, they need to show *and* tell. The process of giving and receiving love, feeling the love, and connecting to the source of love, can lead to a powerful connection between the child and his Creator. Parents' loving care is a child's introduction to her Creator's attributes. It is positive, heart-warming and readily demonstrable.

Al-Wadood is the first among the many attributes of our Creator that we learn to connect vertically. The more we get to know our Creator through learning His attributes, the better equipped we are to make the connection.

Obedience

> So rise, arise, and move the weight of the ego out of sight, so that the good can flow on its natural path unperturbed.[115]

Obedience is an important element to teach a child to connect vertically. Obedience is the manifestation of one's recognition of a true authority. Obedience is a virtue found in all prophets. Prophet Ibrahim and his son Prophet Ismail (peace be upon them both) demonstrated their absolute obedience when Prophet Ibrahim was commanded to sacrifice his son as a test.

The danger of developing the intellect without submitting to divine guidance is like operating a machine without following the instruction manual from the manufacturer. Those endowed with special gifts such as intellect, wealth, strength etc. have a tendency to rely upon their gifts. They depend on their ability to solve problems and to acquire what they want. What our Creator has repeatedly told us to do is to travel and look at what happened to past nations who disbelieved.[116] They were endowed with great strengths and abilities that they thought they were self-sufficient.

Learning and appreciating the Creator's divine attributes both puts us in our place and sets us free at the same time. It frees us from relying on that which elevates all creations when we tame our nafs to submit to the One true sovereignty. Remembrance of the Creator and His infinite attributes is both humbling and empowering. We can do anything for as long as we seek our Lord's guidance and help. He is closer to us than we realise. 'No, my Lord is with me: He will guide me'.[117] Regardless of what we do, God's power is over us, for 'there is no power and no might except by God'.[118]

This can be understood from the position in which one seeks nearness to his Lord. One is closest to his Lord, the Most High when in prostration, i.e., when he lowers his most honourable part of his body—his head onto the ground. The grounding process is necessary for the intellect to expand and to tame the *lower* nafs. Like a ball, it needs to touch the ground before it can bounce up.

Our Creator orders us to firmly establish salaat (formal prayers) in our lives. The minimum unit of prayer requires one to prostrate four times. The daily obligatory prayers alone add up to thirty-four prostrations per day. No other religious constitution requires its members to prostrate this many times each day.

What do all these prostrations do to our prefrontal cortex in the meantime? Neuroscientists discover that the pre-frontal cortex is the location in the brain where inhibition, cognition, reasoning and other higher order thinking processes occur. From a physiological viewpoint, this movement improves blood flow to the prefrontal cortex. It is not a stretch to understand that this part of our brain is frequently and regularly nourished as a result of observing salaat. Muslims have been ordered to observe salaat since it became obligatory in the 8th year of Prophet Muhammad's (peace and blessings be upon him) messenger-ship (around 620CE). We learn that all prophets before him were instructed to prostrate to God in the same manner. Generations of Muslims have obeyed and benefitted without knowing what we know now. In this information era, mounting evidence of Muslim practices in relation to human health should only serve to increase our appreciation for the All-Knowing, the most Merciful.

> If the intellect and the heart move as one, then you can see the light, but if it is the intellect only, the light fades away…. You need more than the little self to keep afloat.[119]

If you desire for your child to reach his potential, the extent of which is known only to his Creator, then set an example of how to be humble and to obey his Lord.

- Model to him what it means to hold the Lord's words as the guiding light in your life. Do not be deluded that man can rely on man's intellect alone
- Explain to your child your rationales of what you tell her. She is likely to listen as long as you strive to live your life accordingly
- Seek guidance from learned people whom you trust
- Have the humility to stand corrected. Human beings are imperfect beings. Accept your child's

challenge when he points out discrepancies between what you say and what you do. Appreciate them as your mirrors. Gracefully accepting correction could be the best example you model to your child yet
- Strive to always practise the Two-Fold, Double-Selection principle in what you do. Align your decisions, your actions, and your words vertically. This teaches your child vertical connection

Vertical Connection—A Pursuit

Whoever directs himself wholly to Allah and does good work has grasped the surest handhold, for the outcome of everything is with God.[120]

There are multiple ways to connect vertically from the Qur'an and Sunnah. I wish to highlight two points here for discussion in terms of vertical connection—the approach and the focus. I will also introduce Circle Connection you can have with your children with a special mention of Sue Roffey's RAPIDS principles. RAPIDS is the acronym of Respect, Agency, Positivity, Inclusion, Democracy, Safety and choice. This is will be explained later in this chapter.

The Approach

Here is an example on what not to do. Several years ago I met Salimah at a gathering organised by a Muslim women's organisation in Perth. Moved by the way an Islamic topic was presented in that gathering, Salimah got a little emotional. She shared her experiences of her own.

Her memories of her ustaadhah (female religious teacher) as a child were mainly about their being cross and stern. The lessons were boring. All she remembered from those classes were rules and punishment. Her relationship with the Qur'an stopped at parroting the Arabic sounds and her progress only went as far as the party her family held for her for having completely read the Qur'an once from cover to cover. Salimah loathed the entire experience. Prior to that Salimah struck a deal with her mother that once she fulfilled her mother's wish to read through the Qur'an, she should not be forced to attend any more lessons after that. She interpreted the process as more for show among her parents' family and friends than to connect with her Creator. For decades she was put off from anything related to Islam.

Sadly, Salimah's experience was not uncommon. Worse still are those who whip their children/students in pursuit of an adult-determined status of success.

We hear of youth suicide in some high-pressure nations from time to time because of disappointing examination results. Competition for success can be taken to an extreme in many nations. What justification can one give when we recall the tragic death of seven-year-old Yaseen in the UK? How he died defies all human reasoning. It was his own mother who beat him to death for not meeting her expectations in memorising the Qur'an![121]

Although an isolated incident, it was one case too many. It takes no convincing to see that the drive behind such behaviour is anything but for the child's best interest. We hope and pray that no child ever suffers such brutality ever again. Unfortunately, corporal disciplining with the cane still happens. Some adults believe that children need this kind of 'tough love'. Young children have no way out but to conform. Adults who get the immediate results are further convinced that this approach works.

Adopting an inappropriate approach to introduce a child to her Creator is not limited to Muslim communities. How one responds to a child's questions about God can have an impact on how this child forms his relationship with God. A friend of mine shares that as a child born into a Catholic family, she was schooled in the convent. She was forever getting into trouble for raising her hand to ask questions about her faith. She was thus labelled as being disruptive in her school reports. By the time she reached her mid-teens, she had had enough and left her religion.

One question begs to be asked: if a stern teacher or meaningless indoctrination could turn a young child off from religion for decades, what kind of seed is planted in a child if corporal punishment is used? Is this appropriate in how a child is introduced to the Merciful Lord and His Divine Guidance? Parents and teachers ought to think long and hard to find ways to help their children make the vertical connection meaningful to them. The ineffective approach an adult takes boils down to one thing: the intense value put on the form, i.e., the observable and quantifiable outcome, rather than the spiritual connection with the divine. I wish to urge parents and teachers to exercise wisdom and compassion in their approach when it comes to teaching, especially religious teachings.

The Focus

If we set our minds to seeking God's pleasure as our goal, we experience a paradigm shift from focusing not merely on the reward but also to value the attainment of peace. The reward is in the future and not entirely in our jurisdiction, whereas a peaceful heart is something we can work for and can be felt more readily. Human beings with our nature and limitations need both—a goal and reassurance along the way.

Parents and teachers when introducing the child to his Creator ought to be clear on what to focus on. To help a young child connect vertically, the initial years should focus more on the concept and love of God, instead of the outer forms and rules of the religious constitution. Call on their in-built angelic nature which has an amazing capacity to respond more than we realise. Lead them in service to others around them. Help them connect with how they feel inside when they share, when they help, when they wait, when they behave with good manners.

Explain in simple terms why they feel the struggle within them when sometimes they do not feel like sharing, not willing to help or wanting immediate gratification. Encourage them and remind them but leave them to choose and learn for themselves. Do not force them to conform, such as prayer and fasting before they reach the legal age. In one of my interviews with parents during my research on parenting Muslims in Australia, a father shared his wisdom that he never forced his daughter to pray. He and his wife prayed and their four year old child would follow from time to time. What he did do was kiss her and praise her for joining them whenever she did participate. Other times she was left to do what she wanted. Repeated positive encouragement gave this young girl all the motivation from within to observe her prayers when she got older. At university, she would take time out for

I'tikaf (secluded worship) during Ramadan. It seemed all so natural to her.

Connection with the Creator is an evolutionary process. Every positive input, however small, will accumulate to something significant in a child's heart. With the right intention to please our Creator, consistency in small doses of positivity we inject into our children carries more weight than an outburst of enthusiasm done once in a blue moon. This means that God, Al-Shakur (the One who is appreciative) is pleased with one's persistent pursuit of good deed, including your concern in your child's connection to Him, irrespective of its size or outcome. Desiring Paradise may be the end goal, but if we do good only for the sake of getting the reward, we tend to forget that our shortcomings can easily jeopardise the outcome. If we do good for seeking God's pleasure, then our understanding and faith in God's attributes and beautiful names will motivate us to keep going without conceit or complacency. For God's pleasure alone surpasses all rewards and happiness. His pleasure is the highest reward in and of itself. We express our gratitude by doing good deeds. Be like the farmer, who works consistently and diligently in hope for a good harvest while accepting the unexpected as it comes. Like farmers, parents know their effort is only part of the means, the rest of their children's growth depends largely on God's intervention and blessing. If one concentrates on the pursuit while leaving the outcome to the Lord, one never fails to be a keen and humble pursuer.

Once when Prophet Muhammad (peace and blessings be upon him) mentioned that someone would be a dweller of the Paradise, he first let his companions know who the person was, then he elaborated on what praiseworthy *action* that particular person did. His key message was not about Paradise, but what the person did consistently. The takeaway message had always been the focus on what type of action as a manifestation of faith. That is the crux of vertical connection.

One setting that is readily available for parents to informally guide their children is Circle Connection.

Circle Connection

Circle Connection is a term I adopted from a framework practised in many education settings. It has been known in the past as Circle Time, Tribes, Learning Circles and more recently, Circle Solutions. Circle Solutions is primarily focused on a strength-based approach in education settings to help children develop problem-solving skills proposed by Sue Roffey.[122]

I propose Circle Connections to help parents help their children connect vertically, internally and externally to attain wellbeing. It is informal, usually more applicable to close family members. It is a circle with an overarching theme of nurturing wellbeing. It is where every member is valued, no judgment is passed, and learning happens spontaneously. Before the invention of television, this was done amongst families in most cultures. In our time, we not only have television to contend with, we now have electronic games and wifi to distract us from bonding with family members. A humorous Minion meme on Pinterest says it all: 'If you want to call a family meeting, just turn off the wifi router and wait in the room in which it is located'. It would not be an exaggeration to say that wifi is a new barrier to family connection in the current information and technology era.

Connection circles used to be everywhere. In Australian Aboriginal literature, for instance, one reads about family members sitting around a campfire in the evenings, listening to the elders' yarns and tales of the Dreamtime. When I visited my father-in-law over fifteen years ago, every night I found everybody, from my father-in-law (the head of the household) to the youngest grandchild, among them the young Burmese girl who was the family's live-in help, all gathered on a piece of rug in the living room around a homemade, portable coal heater. We all sat around watching television shows. Interactions between family members took place during commercial breaks. The best part was when the electricity went out momentarily. That was when the real bonding happened.

This scene transported me back to my own childhood. All credit to my father's insistence on not buying a television, we enjoyed countless circle connections in the evenings around my parents' double bed chatting, laughing, paying each other out, sharing our troubles and thoughts, listening to my father telling us historical events, my mother's recount of her childhood, or their memories of people, events, food of their hometown etc.

One of the most exciting circle connections from memory was when one of my older brothers broke the news to my parents about a girl he was interested in. I remember his hands shaking ever so slightly when he carefully chose his words for that big 'confession'. My other siblings and I sat in pin-drop silence; we latched onto every word he uttered, all the while holding our breath watching our parents' body language from the corner of our eyes. We were all relieved when we saw the soft and warm expression on our parents' faces. Many more circles during that period drew our stickybeaks in with keen interest, until he got married to her a couple of years later. It goes without saying how we delighted at every chance to make our brother blush in between sessions. I saw through the eyes of childish excitement how my parents and brother interacted in making that specific external connection. What was imprinted on me were the principles they held when it came to pursuing a potential life partner and the etiquette that set the tone for establishing a respectful relationship between all parties involved, including the future in-laws.

These casual circles have a way of enabling us to connect with each other, with our past, with our values, with our hearts and with our faith. We learnt so much about manners, about people's emotions, words, body language and what was hidden between the lines all in a fun way around our parents. We never felt we were learning yet the impact had been long-lasting.

Sadly this family circle connection is fast disappearing in our time. Nowadays so many children return to an empty home after school, with no one to ask how their day went, if they had exciting news to share, or if something was troubling them. It is not uncommon to see people take their meals alone in front of the television, or in their own rooms at odd times. It is also not uncommon to notice families sitting together in a restaurant each engrossed in their own electronic devices. In response to a society eroded by 'less stability and more stress in families, more mental illness and addiction…, high levels of social exclusion and a competitive ethos…'[123] Roffey aims at bringing this age-old practice into the classroom. Circle Solution is designed to support children's development of wellbeing, in particular, healthy relationships, resilience in the face of adversity, effective problem-solving skills and responsible behaviour.

You as parents, have this magic circle right there in your hands. To help you appreciate what Roffey's Circle Solution entails, let me share with you her RAPIDS[124] principles I briefly mentioned earlier in the chapter. RAPIDS is an acronym for Respect, Agency, Positivity, Inclusion, Democracy, Safety and choice. These principles, when applied, provide a safe space in which students are coached to find effective ways to solving problems. Although RAPIDS principles are most designed for educational settings, these principles are equally valuable in other coaching settings. Each principle is briefly explained as follows:

Respect

Respect for individuals and their input. One learns respect through experiencing respect.

Agency

Giving students agency helps students to make the shift from a victim mentality to one who believes he/she can effect change. In other words, parents and teachers can find ways to empower a child to find solutions to a problem.

Positivity

An increased sense of belonging raises resilience. It helps students to change from focusing on the problem to focusing on seeking a solution.

Inclusion

Everyone is valued in the circle. Students work with different groups to get to know each other.

Democracy

No one dominates. A fair go for all promotes cooperation.

Safety and Choice

Everyone can watch, listen and learn. No pressure on anyone to speak. Students are more likely to contribute when they feel safe and confident.

You may think that children learning to solve problems from their parents is as natural as breathing. I beg to differ. If this is already happening in your home, you are really blessed. The adults play a vital role in how these circles evolve. My experience may help you see my point. I was doing some deep spring-cleaning recently when I found an A-4 sized exercise book that had Family Meeting Minutes on the cover as its subject. My children and I read a few lines from this book and we were immediately transported down our memory lane over 20 years ago. Within a few minutes we were in stitches from laughing at the expressions, the topics, and the suggestions recorded in that book. Later that day when I had a moment alone to myself, several realisations hit me like a tonne of bricks.

For a start, our circle connections were too formal. Who on earth would have family discussions recorded as meeting minutes? What were we thinking? (There is always a flip side to it: Had I not done it that way, I would not have had the opportunity to reflect on it to share with you now!)

Secondly, the matters discussed were mostly corrective, and not enlightening nor encouraging. The circle connections could do with large doses of positivity.

Thirdly, we now noticed that in the meetings one child was always picked on by another. In order to allow everyone the chance to speak up, we had inadvertently let certain discussions 'exclude' one child. We failed to look out for the safety of that child. Understandably, that child's participation dwindled as was evident in the record—input from this child decreased over time.

Fourthly, the meetings lacked the element of fun. It was not a wonder that these meetings only lasted a few weeks.

Roffey's Circle Solutions are brilliant when these circles are conducted in an education setting. Children in such circles are usually of the same age, in settings with which all are familiar, such as the classroom, the teacher, the rules and the activities in the context they share. Family dynamics are different.

Learning from my experience, I believe the aim of circle connections in a family setting should be for connection rather than for teaching. Parents could share their own experiences and stories, and their insights to Three-Way Connections, discussing and exploring options if anyone had any matters they felt comfortable to discuss in front of the rest of the family, reading positive messages, sharing what we were grateful for, or doing some simple mindfulness exercises.

We could use these circle connection times to plan dinner parties, holidays, what we would like to do for our Eid celebrations, and so on. Calculating our zakat (annual obligatory alms-giving for those who have the means) for example, lends a chance for our children to know how it is worked out, and how we come to decisions of where we distribute our zakat. If time allows follow these circle connections with something fun that everyone could participate, such as a quick board game, sharing a joke, watching a movie together, appreciating artwork etc. The circle connections should be short and sweet to cater for the short attention span of younger children. And everyone is free to leave if they have other matters to tend to.

An organic way to make circle connection happen is to start with your spouse. Make time each day for 'connection' on matters that you want to discuss with each other. It does not have to be a circle in its literal sense. Children are naturally curious. They want to hear everything adults talk about, uninvited. Discreet filtering is necessary. It is a time when you and your spouse spend time talking to each other about family matters. Younger children can play with something on the side. As the children get older, they will listen, interpret and ask questions. From the questions you get a glimpse of what is being processed and what is happening around each child. Gradually the child will express his opinions and apply the wisdom to his context in his unique manner. It is a privilege to be allowed into a child's heart and mind. When it happens it is a window of opportunity for you to mutually share your thoughts.

A few suggestions to your circle connections with your children to consider:

Be Spontaneous

A great time for circle connection is after school, especially if you are the one to pick up your children from school. They usually have a lot to share making the walk/drive home a perfect time to bond. You may notice one child being unusually quiet. You could try to invite this child to participate in the conversation. If she is reluctant, you should make it a priority to connect with her alone later.

As a family, the dining table is a popular place for circle connections to happen. One of the families I interviewed insisted that their children came home for dinner by six. Both parents were working when the children were young. It was almost like a family routine that everyone followed even when after the children were married and had families of their own. As I had the privilege to know them better over the years, the children are very close to their parents and with each other. They have a strong bond that continues to this day.

A time that worked well for me when my children were young was bedtime. It was a time when the children and I were winding down from the day. My husband would join in if he was home early enough. Some nights he would read the bedtime story to the children while I cleaned up after dinner. Once established, it became a natural part of the daily routine. My children always looked forward to sharing that moment with us, being close to us, and listening to our voices reading stories from children's books of their choice, plus our elaborations and animated sounds that helped with their comprehension.

Make it Safe

What made Prophet Muhammad (peace and blessings be upon him) such a great teacher? Apart from divine inspiration, he was lenient and gentle with those around him; for if he did otherwise, people would have run away from him as well as his message.

A welcoming atmosphere promotes learning. The child feels accepted and wants to participate. Your role as parent, storyteller and teacher rolled into one, have the temperature controller in the palm of your hands. When it comes to learning, make sure the setting is pleasant, gentle, lenient, welcoming, encouraging, loving and compassionate. If you manage to have a child come to you willingly, you have achieved 90% of your objective.

Much of our communication is conveyed through our tone of voice and body language. You may choose the nicest words to say, but your non-verbal communication is what will reveal how you really feel at that moment. Do some mindfulness exercise if you have had to transition from a stressful situation before speaking to your child.

Make it Fun

For very young children, using animated voices, their toys or names of people they are familiar with are some of the ways that you can make it relatable and fun for them when you read or tell a story.

Dramatise the scenes. For example, when you read Prophet Yunus (Jonah, peace be upon him) being swallowed by the fish, you could use several layers of blankets and doona to cover up and let your child imagine what it was like being trapped inside the belly of a big fish and how terrified Prophet Yunus must have felt. You can tell the story under the covers in a sad and panicky voice. Children are better at imagining than adults. They will come up with all kinds of things to dramatise the experience. Then let them imagine what it was like to open their eyes to find themselves in the open air on the beach. Use words such as relieved, grateful, remorseful etc. to help them describe the emotions in that moment. Always draw their focus two-fold: from the apparent to what is deeper than the apparent. Then tell them about his response after he was saved.

Keep Them in Suspense

There is nothing more intriguing than being kept in suspense in the middle of an interesting story. Filmmakers and television series producers know this all too well. If you want your audience to stay with you, keep them in suspense at the right moments. You build up their curiosity, you give them a puzzle to mull over, or you bring them to a crossroad, then you leave them there for a moment. You can use this tactic in circle connections with children. You pause at the most exciting part without telling them the ending and ask them to wait till the next evening. Keep your promise and deliver the continuation of the story the next evening… until you arrive at another prime scene where you want to pause again. You do not have to be the best narrators in the world but you can be sure that your children will be most cooperative when it comes to circle connection time. I have heard many children learn to read because they cannot wait till the next session with their parents so they pick up the book to find out for themselves.

Trickle it In

For younger children, choose a time when they are not distracted by unmet biological or emotional needs. Tell them about your elixir of wisdom when they are content and more receptive. Remember to never make the session too long. For older children, watch their body language. Resist the urge to turn a spontaneous teaching opportunity into a lecture.

Do not overkill. Make the most of the first window of their attention. Give them a short sharp reminder, or a quick explanation on the spot. Then stop the urge to go on and on. It is always more effective than a long-winded lecture.

Among the mistakes I made in raising my children was not knowing when to stop. I remember times when my children were still young (when my eldest was under ten years old), I would seize an opportunity to explain to my children something of great value to me. Then in my enthusiasm I would get carried away. You do these enough times, you risk planting selective earplugs in your children each time they hear your voice. It took me some time to detect that glaze over their eyes and immediately realise that my time was up 120 seconds ago!

A professor once shared his wisdom with my husband. He said, 'Respect people's intelligence'. There is nothing worse than stuffing things down people's throat just because you want them to get the nutrition. Let the person get a taste of it, give the person time to digest it. If they want more, be rest assured they will seek it from sources they trust; it does not always have to come from you! The hard truth I learnt from this is, when we overkill, it is no longer about the child, it is our inciting nafs which wants to extend its time on the soapbox.

I have dedicated a good portion of this chapter on

ways to helping children to make the vertical connection. This is because adults' effort to connect vertically for themselves is personal and self-paced; and doing it is a prerequisite. Every individual makes this connection through different means at different times. Strong connection with God is a combination of knowledge, experience and reflection. This does not mean every Muslim parent needs to become a scholar before they can help their children in this respect. It is actually simple. Practise what you know. Seek to gain deeper meaning by implementing what you know. Accumulated personal experience is insight for you and it is yours alone. Engage in Dhikr (remembrance of God) often. Be in the company of those whose presence and actions motivate you to be conscious of God. Make small increments in your good deeds and strive to be consistent. Vertical connection for you is a lifelong pursuit. Vertical connection is the immediate, most reliable, most direct and foolproof measure when parents need support and guidance. It is your ongoing personal development that should happen simultaneously with your parenting, more precisely, parenteering.

In terms of Vertical Connection, I would like to quote a saying of a dear friend who often reminds me that, 'The important thing is that you have planted the seed!' We are only agents. Do not smother the seed too much too early. Since you have been picked for the job of watering and nourishing this child by your Lord, surely you would want to seek guidance and help from your Lord. If you ask, you shall be answered.

CHAPTER EIGHT
Outward/External Connection

When you change the way you look at things,
the things you look at change.[125]

THIS IS THE third part of the Three-Way Connection. We explore the external encounters that cross path with us in life and discuss the way we perceive them, and how we respond to them. How we see them directs our action in how we deal with them. How we deal with them affects our wellbeing. Our goal is to attain the state of ultimate peace and contentment.

Destiny

I often come across the statement which says 'you are in charge of your destiny' in self-help books and motivational talks. This statement is true to a great extent from the perspective of self-determinism. We are given a mind and free will to make decisions for ourselves. We are responsible for our intent, effort and action. We can set a goal, and we utilise and find resources to work towards that goal. Smaller goals lead to greater goals, and hence the sum total of our goals is where our destiny awaits. This generally is true for things within 'our control'.

A Believer's Perspective On Destiny

The statement of 'you are in charge of your destiny' can be easily misinterpreted to mean we will attain *whatever* we set out to achieve and overlook our dependency on the Divine intervention. It overshadows the need for seeking assistance and gratitude in our pursuit. We tend to take our blessings for granted when things are going well. We only have to pause for a moment to realise that there is more to our destiny than just our determination and effort. For starters, being able to wake up alive and healthy every morning is something we cannot guarantee. No one at the beginning of one's journey can say for certain if he will reach his prospective goal. We are completely dependent upon our Lord. Even for the blink of an eye we depend on Him.[126]

The life of Robin Cavendish[127] illustrates how we are completely dependent even for the breath we take. At twenty-eight, Cavendish had much going for him to live a full and productive life. He was first a soldier, then a businessman in tea-brokerage and enjoyed great health. A sudden polio infection left him paralysed from the neck down. Robin's world collapsed overnight. Apart from a strong will and a positive attitude, he was completely dependent, even for every breath he took. Breathing is something we all take for granted yet absolutely crucial to stay alive.

Robin had to rely on a mechanical ventilator that inflated and deflated his lungs for him. For those who reflect there is a sobering message in this story. It is not an exaggeration to say that we owe our entire existence to our Creator and Sustainer. Let us be grateful, beginning with each breath we take. In truth we have little control over what happens around us, or what happens to us in the next minute. We cannot afford not to ask for guidance, protection, and be thankful. Our destiny should be about *our striving* towards our goal to the best of our ability at any given moment, not *the outcome* at which we aim to arrive.

It helps for believers to understand the statement 'in charge of one's destiny' along with being mindful to submitting to the master plan and be grateful for every step we are enabled to take towards our goal. This way you can step out knowing that a safety net is outstretched for you. We have no knowledge except what is revealed to us from the Lord of the universe, including knowledge of the unseen world. The help and opportunities that come to us do not come by chance. What is within our control is to live in hope and to strive hard to arrive at our prospective goal. As for the outcome we hoped to achieve, we have no knowledge to which point we can make it or if we are heading in the right direction at all! We are in need of mercy, guidance and help of our Lord every step of the way.

This approach keeps us in balance—we stay motivated to strive for what is meaningful with the time and means available to us without becoming complacent and arrogant. We live in hope so we work hard and at the same time we accept divine decree to expect anything. In our pursuit of our goals we continue to seek guidance and help and we remain thankful. If we are taken onto a different course, we strive to make the most of the new course. The new course could be a necessary detour to equip us better to achieve what we set out to achieve in the first instance. The new course could also take us onto a completely different path that is ultimately better for us. The new course could even be the turning point that we did not know we needed in order to be saved from heading to our own ruins. We must accept whatever unplanned encounters that cross our paths.

If we change our perspective of our life goals, ambitions, or achievements, to arrive at a peaceful heart when we meet our Creator, then it really does not matter what we do or where we end up, as long as we strive to please our Creator. No one can take away that peace.

The means to attain peace is through actions that take us nearer to our Creator. Ibn Qayyim says, 'He who keeps his heart near God will find peace and tranquillity, whilst he who gives his heart to the people will find restlessness and apprehension.'[128] On our journey home, we strive for tranquillity of the heart at every crossroad, every turn, every rise and every fall. This is because a troubled heart is always harder to bear than physical hardship. Prophet Yusuf (Joseph, peace be upon him) would rather choose imprisonment than to succumb to his treacherous mistress's scandal.[129] Prophet Ayyoub (Job, peace be upon him) remained patient while bearing the distress of prolonged illness and pain of losing his children.[130] His only invocation to God was:

> Suffering has truly afflicted me, but You are the Most Merciful of the merciful. We answered him, removed his suffering, and restored his family to

him, along with more like him, as an act of grace from Us and a reminder for all who serve Us.[131]

The paths that the above two prophets opted for were by no means a walk in the park. Despite it being difficult, their choice was for the same goal—to accept whatever test was decreed for them seeking purity and closeness to their Lord, to attain the ultimate success. Let us take a look at a range of creations and encounters in life. Our perspective on how we see them can affect in how we manage them.

Creations And Experiences Explained

What I mean by outward connection, in a nutshell, is our perspectives on creations other than the self that we come across in life, and how we relate/respond to them.

Creations Other Than The Self

Creations include everything other than the Creator. Creations can be concrete or abstract to our sensory faculties.

Concrete Creations

Concrete creations have characteristics that our senses can perceive. A house is a concrete creation. Body tissues, limbs, sensory organs etc. are concrete creations. A tree, a river, an animal, family, friends, acquaintances or enemies are all creations other than the self.

Abstract Creations

The body systems, intellect, emotions and the *abilities* to hear, smell, touch, see and taste are creations of abstract nature. The sensory organs are the concrete vehicles through which the abstract abilities are transpired. Sight in a living creation is abstract while the eye is concrete. No one can flick a switch to make a child's lungs inflate at birth. No one can stop another person from thinking. Scientists have identified the site in which intellectual activities take place but we only make assumptions of *how* learning happens. That ability is abstract. We gain knowledge of what our body systems do from centuries of diligent observation, studies and research. Why the brain works the way it does and why the digestive system works the way it does is not explainable unless one believes everything exists and operates according to the precise design and will of the One whose creative power is far beyond any creation's comprehension; not even the human intellect.

Energy

Examples of other forms of abstract creations include energies from the wind, electricity, magnet or heat and what they can do. We cannot see wind but we believe it exists when we notice our clothes flap, our skin feels the change in temperature, we see leaves flying and we hear the whistling. These are clues, or signs that tell us a wind is blowing our way. Scientists may be able to tell us what the brain can do and where a particular function takes place, they have studies as far as the route of how electrical impulses are conducted, yet no one can explain why it is not the digestive organ that does this job. As creations we are merely able to observe the created, make connections of what is observed, and notice patterns of the existing systems in place. We are not able to fully comprehend, let alone explain all things.

Creations of the Unseen

Some creations are created on a different frequency to humans and they seldom cross path with us. Therefore, no concrete evidence can be collected to convince sceptics of their existence, except one who believes in what has been revealed by the Creator. One of the articles of faith for Muslims is to believe in creations of the unseen. These creations are veiled from our eyes in this earthly life. Examples of such creations are many, such as paradise, hellfire, angels and jinn. We learn about their existence from the Creator's words, i.e., the Qur'an, and what was revealed to Prophet Muhammad (peace and blessings be upon him). Occasionally a person may be given the ability to see some of these creations,[132] but they are the exceptions to the overwhelming majority.

Here I would like to elaborate a little on angels and jinn. Angels are created from light.[133] They are created to obey and carry out God's commands. Different angels carry out different duties. Angel Gabriel is responsible for bringing messages from the Creator to His chosen prophets. We also believe each person has angels appointed to protect, and to record everything one says and does although they are veiled from our sight. We are also informed that angels join circles of people's gatherings whenever God's names are remembered and mentioned.[134] They make supplications for the believers.

We also learn from our Creator that the jinn are another form of creation made from smokeless fire. The jinn live parallel lives as humans. They have families and they have been given the ability to choose between good and evil. The believing jinn submit to and worship God.[135] They know not to cross bounds with humans. However, the head of the evil jinn (collectively known as Satan)—Iblees—disobeyed God's command to bow down to Adam (peace be upon him). Iblees and his offspring were doomed to Hellfire forever because of his arrogance and stubbornness.[136] He made a vow to God that he and his offspring would do everything they could to bring as many humans as possible to hell with them. Since then began humans' continuous battles against Satan until the Day of Judgment.[137]

Experiences

Experiences include events, situations, moments etc. that we experience. They can be concrete or abstract.

Concrete Experiences

When someone speaks to you, this interaction is a concrete experience. When you have a fall, this incident is a concrete experience. When you attend an event, the proceedings of the event are concrete experiences to you. In other words, experiences that are from concrete creations in our perceptions are Concrete Experiences.

Abstract Experiences

Abstract experiences are phenomena people experience which few others share. These experiences are mostly subjective. They are real to the ones who experience them. Emotions, intuitions, ideas, for example, are abstract experiences.

As was mentioned in the previous paragraphs, like people, there are good as well as evil jinn. Some people may have encounters with jinn and may even have gotten glimpses of them. To those who do not believe in their existence, these experiences are dismissed as people's overactive imagination, hallucinations or make-beliefs out of superstitions. Even among some Muslims, these experiences are looked upon with a degree of scepticism.

Although these occurrences are rare, it has been recorded that people can experience them. Prophet Muhammad (peace and blessings be upon him), who was sent to mankind as a role model, fell ill from someone inflicting black magic on him. This is a demonstration to believers that, one, this species of creation exists, and two, no one is immune to these unseen creatures' evil. In some collections of authentic Hadiths there had been recorded incidences where people interacted with jinn in their lives. Some were left unharmed while others endured various degrees of ill effects.

Fortunately for believers we believe no harm is to exist without God having created a cure for it. For those who believe and make the effort to implement what has been taught, there are instructions from the Qur'an and Sunnah of Prophet Muhammad (peace and blessings be upon him) for protection against the evil of Satan.

I wish to remind my readers that no human beings are immune from the influence of Satan, who incites them to indulge in their lower desires, leads them to commit excess, or to sin. Many recommended practices, if adhered to, are there for believers to seek protection in God from the influences of such promptings. This has been elaborated in more detail in chapter six on Inward Connection. The paragraphs below discuss our responses to external creations and experiences, which collectively, I call them External Encounters.

Dealing With External Encounters

Every day we make multiple decisions related to external encounters that cross paths with us. Understanding the nature of the creations and experiences from a wellbeing perspective allows us a lens to view them with some clarity. Each encounter triggers responses from us. Our chosen responses to these encounters are our outward, or external connections, or in some cases, disconnections. If we are well connected inwardly, and are striving to be in the habit to connect vertically, our responses to these external encounters can become the means to serve our overall wellbeing. This is using our Outward Connections to *close the loop* for our ultimate wellbeing. I will elaborate on closing the loop later in this chapter.

Sometimes we come across unpleasant external encounters that we cannot avoid. A few examples include being laid off at work, being diagnosed with cancer, being hit by a car or having to face the death of our loved ones. God tells us that

> We shall certainly test you with fear and hunger, and loss of property, lives and crops. But [Prophet], give good news to those who are steadfast, those who say, when afflicted with a calamity, 'We belong to God and to Him we shall return.' These will be given blessings and mercy from their Lord, and it is they who are rightly guided.[138]

We connect deeply with people we trust and love. We disconnect resolutely from those who betray or threaten our wellbeing. Sometimes several encounters hit us all at once that force us to make quick decisions. The more insightful we are with ourselves, the calmer we are at dealing with these external encounters. The stronger our vertical connection, the clearer it is to see our priorities. The more we are tested, the more we learn and reflect, and these become useful tools to manage future encounters. This process of connecting in three ways continues throughout one's entire life. It is an ongoing cycle of learning, unlearning or re-learning. Each experience adds to the dimensions and layers of our Three-Way Connection. The following subsections discuss the ways in which to connect externally to an external stimulus, be it a creation or an occurrence.

Outward Connection As A Means To Attain Wellbeing

This chapter focuses on our perspectives of various creations and encounters with which we interact to help us enhance or maintain our state of wellbeing. Creations and encounters that cross paths with us can be broadly categorised as blessings and tests. In many instances we can exercise our free will to connect or disconnect from external encounters. Every day we make such decisions whether we realise it or not. I have summed up five key practices to deal with external encounters:

- detach
- accept the second fold
- value the pursuit not the outcome
- find meaning in what you do, and
- practise spiritual hygiene

Detach

While connecting with things or people we love is easy, dealing with the devastation or severe sadness when losing them is hard. Yet all things created on earth will perish. To save us the heartbreak from excessive attachment we need to learn to put things in their right perspective so we can detach. Having a tool or two and consistent practice can help us detach.

Losing your favourite things can be upsetting. If we see the loss as a form of training to detach, then the loss becomes our gain. Remember we are on our one-way journey home. The things we become attached to will either eventually leave us, or we will leave before them when our time on Earth ends. Excessive attachment to any creation is a hindrance to our peaceful return. Therefore, our merciful Lord gives us doses of losses to prepare us to yearn to attach to the everlasting. Over the years I picked up a saying from my husband whenever one of us had an object broken, or even when our beloved cat was run over in our street. His expression 'even people die' quickly puts things in perspective for me. This reminder has become an effective detachment tool for me. Keeping good company and having mental preparation are two ways to help one detach.

Keeping Good Company

Be in the company of those who reminds you to see the bigger picture. Once a friend of mine went overseas with her husband to visit family for a month. Her anxiety level hit the roof when one day her daughter called to inform her that she found her freezer door left open. The daughter had to bury the freezer-full of rotten food in her garden. When this friend thought about what damage this would have done to the expensive flooring of her new house she became listless. Luckily her level-headed husband put her at ease. He told her to enjoy her time with her family. He explained that things could always be replaced. Material things could never compare with precious time spent with family. Besides, worrying could not help the situation. Her anxiety about the situation was instantly relieved. Sometimes all we need is for someone to remind us to see the bigger picture. Family and friends can do this for each other.

Mental Preparation

Mental preparation is another method to help us detach, especially from things that you tend to place importance, be they people, things, or ideals. Take people, for example. No matter how much we love a person, we need to be mindful that this person's journey may end at any time, just like our own. Losing our loved ones is never easy, especially if the one you lost is your child. This is where faith can give you buoyancy when you feel you would drown in pain over the loss.

Accept The Second Fold

Rumi was quoted to have said that 'the wound is the place where the Light enters.'[139]

The Apparently Bad

Bad things happen for good reasons. What appears in front of us may later reveal something totally different. External encounters that are seen as apparently 'bad' such as accidents, loss of wealth, project disasters, etc., are not something we would volunteer for, but they happen. They happen for good reasons. There is a prayer Muslims say whenever they hear of someone is sick to say 'Don't worry, it will be a purification for you, Allah willing.'[140] This makes one mindful that no afflictions will touch a believer without his/her soul being purified by God. Falling sick appears to be suffering, but it is a purification of one's soul from God.

At times we come to a dead end in our pursuits and had it not been for the dead end we would never have forced ourselves to think outside the square to find solutions or even outcomes we never imagined possible. Sometimes interruptions to our plans turn out to be just what we needed to build our character strengths such as patience, tolerance, resilience and grit that stretch our capacity to hold blessings reserved for us around the corner. Difficulties force us to grow. Deaths of loved ones remind us to check and repack what goes into our bags for our final journey home.

The Apparently Good

Good people in our lives, like good fortune, are tests too. The people we love are tests while they are with us and more so after they leave us. While they are with us, we can become so emotionally invested that we look at them with rose-coloured lenses that make us lose our fair judgment because of them. We can become so consumed by our attachment to them that we lose our minds over their absence.

Wealth, power, position etc. are things that people covet but they can also destroy a person. If we plant them in our hearts and let them take root, we might fail the test. This is because what goes into our hearts stays. God says in the Qur'an:

> Wealth and children are the attractions of this worldly life, but lasting good works have a better reward with your Lord and give better grounds for hope.[141]

Lessons We Learn

Remember all creations will cease to exist at some point. What would you do if the post you leaned on suddenly snapped? You would want to grow wiser by looking for something permanent and strong that can carry your weight! Connecting vertically at a time like this re-directs us to turn towards the One who is everlasting and truly dependable. Losing someone you always depended upon forces you to seek strength from within, and from the One who strengthens. It could be a blessing in disguise if you are made to realise the need to re-evaluate on whom you should really depend. Shift your dependency from someone/something to the Creator of all creations. When you ask for help, ask the One on whom all creations depend. Lean on the One who is Almighty, who is Eternal, who is the Lord and Giver of Mercy, the One who will always be there for you.

Some encounters and creations are there to support, guide, protect, comfort and help us. Some encounters and creations are opportunities for us to give back. Still some encounters and creations grind on our nerves to get the rough edges out of us. We learn what to do from certain situations and we learn what not to do from others. When we begin to consider everyone and everything is placed along our path for a specific purpose, the energy we use to connect with them will shift.

Value The Pursuit, Not The Outcome

When it comes to external encounters that are worthy of our effort, we can turn every moment into a means of worship with the sole intention to please God. We put in our best effort even though the task seems boring or trivial. Others may hijack your idea. There are times when people may take credit for your efforts. Promising progressions may go pear shape or come to a dead end after years of investment of finances, time and energy. We need to remember that we are held accountable only for the intention and action we take throughout the process. Whether we live to see the outcome, or if we are able to arrive at its completion is not in our jurisdiction. It is the pursuit of what we pack into our bags for our journey home that counts. Bear in mind that:

- No intention goes unaccounted
- No deed goes in vain
- No hurt afflicts a believer but he is purified

Find Meaning In What We Do

Knowing your purpose on Earth gives you the anchor to hold onto what is worth connecting to. During one of the interviews for my research on parenting, one participant shared an interesting comment his colleague made. He said that religious practices were more likely to pass on to future generations than cultural practices among migrants. Propagation of cultural practices is dependent upon people of the same culture wanting the same ritual to continue. Many migrant groups gradually lose some of their cultural practices among their second and third generations in their host countries. Religious practices, if passed on for preserving cultural traditions, will face a similar fate as some of the migrant cultures, unless these practices are taught with an understanding as a means to strengthen a person's relationship with his Creator. A change of place of residence should not be an influential factor in the latter case.

Practising religion for the right reasons gives people meaning in what they do. It helps them to resist cultural impositions or pressure to conform for the sake of preserving social norms or to protect their family reputation. We experience less anxiety if we do away with people's expectations. We become less affected by people's opinions of us. We are less affected by negative peer pressure. Instead, we strive to channel our focus on seeking the pleasure of God. We are less burdened by what people think of us. I feel this is particularly important for parents because so many children rebel against conforming to traditions that make no sense to them. If the authority to practise comes from the Creator and not any creation, then the matter is simplified.

Practise Spiritual Hygiene

Incorporate spiritual hygiene practices into your life. They are similar to the sound practices to maintain our physical health such as frequent hand-washing, regular bathing, adequate sleep, nutritious food, dental and personal hygiene, etc. For our spiritual hygiene, there are daily morning and evening supplications from the Sunnah, as well as frequent words of remembrance of God that teach Muslims to seek purification of the soul.

Prophet Muhammad (peace and blessings be upon him) also recommended practices and supplications to boost our immunity against influences of the evil beings. For no creation can escape the Divine Power. 'Flee to God' expresses the urgency for believers to connect with our Creator. Fleeing normally means to run away *from* something fast. Here the expression used in the Qur'an is 'flee **to** God', meaning we need to get away from the devils and *run to* God, the one who can really protect us. In this sense, even the devils on earth are a form of test for believers.

Connect Outwardly To Close The Loop For Wellbeing

Here I would like to elaborate on what I mentioned earlier in this chapter about closing the loop for our ultimate wellbeing. When an external creation or encounter crosses path with us, our response—whatever it is—will boomerang back to us. Most of the time we reap what we intended and the way we responded. Choose wisely with whom, what and how you connect in order to close the loop to return to your Lord in peace.

Covey suggests that between a stimulus and response, there is a space.[142] Within this space is where human beings exercise their unique abilities of self-awareness, imagination, conscience and independent will.

Our self-awareness, imagination and conscience are tools to help us assess and predict the dynamics of our interactions with the external creations and encounters. The freedom to choose allows us to determine if and how we connect or disconnect with these encounters. On-going practice to connect inwardly and vertically increases our awareness, knowledge and wisdom when it comes to interacting with the external creations and encounters.

Your decision becomes easy if you serve only One being. As mentioned earlier, all creations will perish. If your purpose in life is to serve them, you will be alone when their time is up. If you depended on any of them, you will be let down. No creation is absolutely dependable because they themselves are dependent. Choose to lean on the One who is dependable and is always there for you; the One who does not tire, who does not need to rest, who is ever-living.

Acrobats can perform effortlessly in air not because they were born with the skills and had no fear, but because of their repetitive routine that made them skilful and the countless number of falls have built in them a trust, knowing the safety measures are in place. As mentioned earlier, faith and your vertical connection habits will give you buoyancy when you are being tested. What I mean by buoyancy is during times of trial, your regular practice is what will keep you afloat. You will experience all the hardship and emotional turmoil as everyone else, but you have an extra sense of trust to accompany you. This is because your regular wellbeing practice has given you 'air' that will bring you back up sooner than you know. This 'air' is a mix bag of intangible spiritual connection with your Creator, of trust, submission, hope, patience and acceptance deep within you.

Your regular practice to occupy yourself with remembrance and prayer will put you in safe mode when tested. You may plummet into a state of severe anxiety, panic attack, depression or despair, but hopefully not for too long. You shift your focus onto what you can do. Your habits to connect vertically will kick in to channel your energy to ask for forgiveness, mercy, help and protection. As devastating as it may be, you accept whatever is to unfold before you. As a result, you will come out having being renewed, strengthened, and refined. You gain deeper understanding of who you really are.

Trials teach you to detach from the created. The more you detach from the created, the more you connect with your Creator. You gain new appreciation for your Creator in the gift of time, health and opportunities you have right now. You reassess your preparation for your return journey. You unpack, purge and repack what you wish to bring to your final destination. It is a process that takes a lifetime to evolve. The process continues until you breathe your last. Let that be how you practised the Three-Way Connections because you honoured the soul within you.

Your actions are what your children will remember. Modelling the ultimate wellbeing practice takes years and it need not be many; perhaps a handful of habits will serve them a long way. My parents always lived by example to spend within their means. No matter how difficult life got for them financially, they never borrowed from people. They made do with what little they had. They worked harder. They taught us to do without. This had been such a valuable wellbeing principle for us up till now, of which I hope to pass onto my children and their future generations.

Children As An External Encounter

This book is about your wellbeing as parents. This chapter is about attaining wellbeing through external connection. I would like to dedicate the remaining pages of this chapter to look at our children in terms of our external connection for our wellbeing.

What is your view of children? Do you see children as gifts, responsibilities, burdens, means for growth or means for heartbreaks for you? I have provided a range of parental perspectives concerning children. These perceptions have no right or wrong. Each person's perspective is unique, shaped by their individual experiences and socialisation. Which of the following resonates with your connection with your children?

Seven Varying Parental Perspectives Concerning Children

Children as Gifts

Children are seen as adornments for parents in this life. They bring happiness and they make the family unit feel complete. They give parents the opportunity to love unlike any other. Children are parents' pride and joy. In certain cultures, larger number of children represent prosperity and power.

Children as Responsibilities

No matter which culture you come from, parents are responsible for their children's care, growth and wellbeing. Universally parents are responsible for at least the first several years of their children's lives when they are completely dependent and vulnerable. These are times when children rely on adults to care for them until they gradually gain skills to become independent. Responsibilities of parents over their children change as they get older. Different societies and cultures differ in their views of the age when a child is considered to have reached adulthood.

Children as a Burden

Some parents who have unresolved issues or for various other reasons may see their children as obstacles to living a life they had wanted for themselves. Those who are experiencing difficulties in life, such as financial strains, relationship issues or various health issues may regard their children as having compounded their hardship, misery and anger. Children with illnesses, mental or physical disorders, are a big challenge to the parents' relationship with each other, and can become a strain on parents' energy, time, emotions, resilience, and resources.

Different societies have different norms on how long parents should provide shelter for their children. A few years after we migrated to Australia, my husband attended a public speaking workshop. All participants were asked to share what they had achieved during the week. One participant proudly announced that he and his wife finally *kicked their 20-year-old son out of the house*! The audience applauded but my husband was stunned. Being brought up in a collectivist society where parents were expected to provide shelter for all unmarried children, he struggled to appreciate the humour in that man's statement. To this day he still remembers the cultural shock he experienced in that moment!

Children as a Means for Growth

Since parenting is a completely hands-on job, different stages of your children's development pose different challenges that push your boundaries. If you have the mindset of a parenteer and admit that you too are finding your way in your role, these challenging experiences will definitely change you, making you stronger and wiser.

Children as an Investment

Some parents, generally those who grow up in collectivist cultures tend to expect their children to support them when they get old. In certain places, children are seen as an economic means for the family. Muslim parents hope that their children will pray for them after they die and benefit from the boomerang effect of what they imparted to their children.

Children as a Cause for Heartbreaks

One of the most heart-wrenching tests a person can experience is witnessing their children on the road to self-destruction, be it morally, mentally or physically. Parents in such situations experience much fear, anxiety, shame, helplessness, not to mention heartbreak. I once worked with a lady whose son unfortunately had an addiction to illicit substances. The way she described each break-in to her house really broke my heart. She almost sounded like she was numb from her son's abuse whenever he was desperate for money to get a fix.

Children are with Us on Loan

Any loan is a trust. Viewing children as a loan allows us to acknowledge absolute ownership to the rightful owner, our Creator. Like a book you borrowed from the library, you would take care to keep it clean, not to let water spill over it, not to dog-ear its pages, and never to scribble in it. You know if you did, there are consequences to follow. The same goes for your children. The length of the loan term is unknown. Parents who see their children through this perspective would want to make every minute they have with them meaningful and joyous. This view brought about a great paradigm shift for me.

I am sure you will not agree with all of the perspectives

mentioned above. There is no way I could cover all possible perspectives that exist. For example, in some traditions that believe in karma where one's actions affect the cycle of rebirths, they believe that the family one is born into is ultimately determined by one's actions in the past lives. This is outside the realm of our discussions. I have only put forward a few perspectives to encourage readers to examine their external connections with their children.

Connecting With Your Children

Your perspective of your children determines how you connect with them. I have summed up five pointers for parents to be mindful of when you make that connection.

As I had intended for this book to be one that shares what *I wish I had known* back when I was a young parent, I have the following suggestions to share with young parents from my personal experience:

- You are not defined by your children
- You are your child's first school
- Your children's paths are not yours to meddle with
- Maintain a healthy relationship with your children, and
- Be a means to your child's wellbeing

You are Not Defined by Your Children

I was a bit of a dragon mum in my younger days. I went from thinking 'I need my children to be perfect' to believing 'My children's shortcomings are a direct reflection of who I am'. I kept playing these two narratives in my head. I went to all measures to ensure no one criticised my children. I was strict with their manners. I took everyone's comment personally and analysed every non-verbal gesture from people. As hard as it was for me to admit, my energy came from a less wholesome place within. I was not wrong to want the best for my children: sound character, good manners, education and all. However, my driving force came from the wrong place. Completely unaware, I was parenting my children like a confused show-horse trainer, not the kind of trainer who tamed and guided for the benefit of the horse.

I am grateful to have been able to view my mixed-up motives differently over the years. If some prophets were given both righteous and disobedient children, how is anyone else immune to such tests? I have learnt to separate who I am from how my children turn out. They are a part of me but they are not all of me. Likewise, I am a part of them but I am not the only influence on whom they will become. I am an individual with my unique experiences and insights quite different from anyone else, my children included. As a young parent I did not have the skills to look inwardly, nor was I suitably connected vertically to be able to see my connection with my children this way.

You are Your Child's First School

Children's rapid learning occurs not in school but in the first five years of their lives from their caregivers and home environment. They absorb and learn to make connections with things at an astounding rate during this period. The following suggestions are provided for your reference to help your children learn.

Perspectives on Mistakes. If you regard mistakes as opportunities to gaining valuable building blocks to learning, then your children are likely to want to take on new challenges in the future and not be crippled by fear of failing. Ever heard of performance anxiety? Many children have anxieties around performance at school. Anxiety impedes learning. Performance suffers if a child is anxious. It is a vicious cycle. Creating a safe learning environment that celebrates effort rather than the outcome not only facilitates learning, it sets the tone for a healthy learning attitude in your child.

Children are born to learn. Your attitude towards *achievement*, and the flip side of the same coin, *failure*, makes a world of difference in your child's attitude towards learning. Praise their *effort* instead of the result. Encourage them to learn through trial and error. Do not jump in to assist them unless they ask for it. Maria Montessori says, '… the child's individual liberty must be so guided that through his activity he may arrive at independence… the child who does not do, does not know how to do.'[143] Celebrate effort that brings about incremental changes in their development, however small these may seem.

Learn Through Play. Children are naturally curious about everything in the world. They learn much through play. Provide age-appropriate activities and let them explore. Delay young children's exposure to digital gadgets. Minimise electronic gadgets and digital screen time. Resist the urge to buy them too many toys. Create hands-on opportunities for them to explore the world around them. The iconic Australian children's educational program Play School has been around for fifty years.[144] It calls on children's imagination, it teaches children to make props and toys using everyday recyclable materials. Programs like Play School provide parents with endless ideas to keep pre-school aged children occupied while they learn through play.

Establish Good Learning Habits. Habit is something that one does often in a repeated way until it has become a part of their life. Good habits in children take adults a great deal of patience and repetition to establish.

Take schoolwork for example, set aside a specific place and specific time every day for them to complete their work before they can go off to play. Have all the stationery and essential tools such as dictionary, thesaurus, world atlas etc. handy so they do not have excuses to go in and out of the study area. Place all necessary stationery in a box in the centre of the table/desk where your children do their homework. Remove distractions from the learning area. Teach your children to keep this area clean, neat and quiet especially if the child has to share the space with other siblings.

Take your children to the library frequently and read to them every day. Every child should have a library card and you can guide them to choose books, videos, CDs etc. Enjoy the books with your children. This way they are likely to develop the love of reading for life. These stories lend parents great resources to use as examples when you teach them new concepts. A love for reading opens up the world to your children for the rest of their lives.

Assign Chores. Assign duties for them to serve the family. My mother aced this because for some unknown reason that to this day, my favourite kitchen duty is still washing up! My other job in grade two was to polish everyone's shoes on weekends. I did not particularly like the job to start with. But over time I took pride in the shiny shoes on the shoe shelf. Thanks to my parents who instilled in us a sense of responsibility and pride in giving service to others, I learnt that my service started with taking care of my family.

Seize Learning Opportunities. Learning is not limited to schoolwork. Due to our dietary guidelines, reading the ingredients on labels when we go shopping is like second nature to us. The children learn early on to differentiate items that are permissible from the impermissible from the ingredient list. These days most supermarkets provide the standard unit price for their products for people to compare. This was not the case when my children were growing up so they learnt to use mental mathematics to compare prices for value just by following me around when I did my shopping. Back in the days when every car had a street directory, my primary school-aged children learnt to direct me to their sports ground or friends' houses because they had a vested interest in this process. This prepared them to work out their orientation from 2-D maps, reading coordinates on Cartesian planes later in school without difficulties.

Involve them in planning family events such as holidays, special celebrations and dinner parties. You may be delighted at discovering a budding organiser among your children as in the case of our youngest child. She could barely spell when she started to enthusiastically 'write' me to-do lists as soon as we talked of a holiday. She used to take pride in writing up my shopping list before we headed to the supermarket.

Your Children's Paths are Not Yours to Meddle with

One liberating fact that gave me oxygen as a parent was that our connection with our children is, after all, from one creation to another. We have certain guardianship responsibilities but we can never, nor do we have the right to carve out their paths for them the way we want. Besides, how could we know what that path is?! Their paths are designed by our Creator, the Master planner.

Each child is an individual whose soul belongs to the One who created it. The parents' job includes but is not limited to looking out for, nurturing, coaching and helping them to establish strong values and good character. Parents expose children to learning opportunities, help them establish good learning habits, and spot their individual strengths, interests and natural tendencies. Model the kind of behaviour you want your children to have. Appeal to their internal compass to differentiate right from wrong. Respect and appreciate their natural desire to learn and grow. These desires are inbuilt in every child. Be the parent who nurtures and helps to develop these abilities to sprout into seedlings, then saplings, and watch and marvel at what comes out after that. With some guidance, what career they choose to take up in life is their choice. Make their happiness and fulfillment in what they do your objective, instead of a specific career path you want them to take.

Nurture Your Relationship with Your Children

Your relationship with your children is the thread that keeps you connected with them. Therefore, strive to NEVER sever this connection, even when you think you are at the end of your wits. Your children will be your test at one point or another. What to do if you are faced with such tests?

Stay Calm. Staying calm is easier said than done, especially when your children reach adolescence. They suddenly become opinionated, rebellious, they demand more rights, not to mention their crabby unstable moods and even behaving rudely at times. Minimise confrontation as much as you can but do not condone their inappropriate behaviour. Learn to read their mood, their body language and their receptiveness to you. Be tactful and look for the right time and opportunity to speak to them. Allow yourself time to process and figure out the best way to broach the subject about a specific behaviour you want them to think through. Check your own emotions before you speak with them. Do not blame, do not shame and do not label. Rather, be direct about their behaviour. Explain the impact of their behaviour on those around them. Encourage them to find ways to improve. How you connect with them can make all the difference in shaping their attitude and behaviour in life. Keep the growth mindset in mind. Like us, they too, are a work in progress.

Grow with Them. The thing I learnt through raising my children is that you must grow with your children. The hardest task is to adjust yourself to the multiple changes in your first child when he/she goes through his/her growing pains. Their changes can come to you like a shock to your system because you never imagined what it would be like until it hit you. Hang in there. It is a phase they go through.

Read up about the changes an adolescent child undergoes to help you understand why your once obedient, placid and cooperative child turned into a grizzly gruff bear overnight. They are undergoing a major phase of transitioning from a child to an adult. Their hormones are doing a lot of the work. The changes are all happening so fast that they themselves cannot even get a grip on them. Try to see the way they see the world, give them freedom but set boundaries. Hold them accountable to their behaviour and give them space to express their viewpoints. Listen with empathy. Listen in between the lines.

An understanding and tolerant parent can soften the blow of adolescence on both parent and child. At least as an adult you can do your bit to minimise conflict between you and your adolescent child. We live in an ever-changing world. Parents cannot afford to stay in a time warp. If you do you are forgoing your opportunity to connect with your children during a critical phase of their lives. This is happening everywhere. Parenting in the 21st Century is very different to parenting in the 1960s.

For migrant parents, parenting is much more complicated than parents who have lived in the same society for generations. In my studies I learnt that most young people find it difficult to communicate with their parents due to differences in thinking, perspectives, language and parenting approach. My studies focused on parenting and wellbeing support for Muslim children in Australia, a pluralistic social context. Most of the participants I interviewed were migrants from collectivist societies. School counsellors in Muslim schools revealed many issues associated with the gap between young people and adults who were stuck in a context not always applicable to their children's lives.

You as parents have a duty to help your children develop their identity in the new society. You cannot possibly understand exactly what they have to contend with on a daily basis. You may not know how you can assist them. The least you ought to do is to have empathy. Do not insist that you know better because you yourself are not totally versed in your adoptive society. What you can do is learn with your children. Grow with them. Try and see things from your children's perspective with an open mind.

Keep the Door of Communication Open. Impose less, listen more. Often times without extended family support, we as parents are everything to our children. Use less of the authoritarian approach. Instead, using diplomacy, humour, and not seeking immediate compliance can go a long way in your relationship with your children especially as they get older.

Instead of blurting out what is on your mind, choose your words carefully and filter out at least 50% of what you intended to say to them. Remember: *Less is More.* Your silence can be more powerful than a truckload of ranting. Give your children the chance to reflect and correct their mistakes. They want to feel that you trust them enough to use their ability to choose wisely. In most cases, children will not want to lose this trust. At times they may have their own reasons for not complying. Give them the opportunity to explain. Seek to understand their viewpoint.

If you strive to keep the door of communication open, they are likely to let you in when they are ready. I have had a fair share of arguments and blowouts with my children in their adolescent years. I have learnt to apologise to them after I sorted out my own emotions. It was not easy at first. The more you practise the easier it gets. In doing so, you not only take the initiative to mend your relationship, you also model to your children what to do when they realise they are in the wrong. I am proud of them, because until now they have not failed to come back to apologise for their mistakes.

Be There for Them. When they are ready to open up, be all ears for them. These are precious moments you do not want to miss. The more you make yourself available to them and make it safe for them to talk, the more they will open up.

Despite all my inadequacies and misalignments, this is one area I am at peace with myself. Since their father is away most of the time, I make myself available to them to the best of my ability. Sometimes they will turn up at the least convenient times, like twelve midnight when you are already late for bed. For what it is worth I believe it was my availability and willingness to listen that kept the lines of communication open between my children and me. Even when they seem unapproachable, convey your love to them in their primary love language to let them know you are there for them.

Be prepared for unpleasant conversations. Sometimes older children want to say to you things that are difficult for you to hear. We all have our blind spots. How you react will determine if they will ever want to talk about it with you again. As hard as it is to be confronted with your own blind spots, appreciate how difficult it is for your children to tell you to your face the things you do not like hearing, but necessary for you to hear regardless! Listen attentively. You may not be able to digest it straight away, but listen anyway. Take your time to think it through. A lot of the times they do have a point.

Learn to Negotiate. As children get older, they want to explore and exert their rights and expand their influence. Listen to their pleas and compromise within reason when necessary. The saying 'pick your battles and win the war' really has age-old wisdom when applied to parenting young adults.

Let Go. Letting go is one of the hardest things parents have to do. But let go you must. When they try to push your boundaries, openly discuss your concerns and assess the situation *with* your child. Negotiate an agreeable term to meet them halfway. Brainstorm alternatives with your child. Picture your child as one who is attempting to leave behind the training wheels of her bike can make the letting go process a little less frightening. She will wobble and sway at the beginning. Celebrate the fact that she is about to begin her new discovery of the big world out there. You would rather that they made mistakes while you were around so you could guide and support them than not learning how to manage the hard facts of life at all.

Our son, upon finishing high school, insisted on going away with a few of his non-Muslim friends to their group's own School Leavers' trip. His father and I did not want him to go for many reasons, the main reason being it was in Ramadan. He pleaded and debated with us to let him go. In the end we agreed to take the advice from a religious scholar. Our son chose a young scholar to consult with. We ended up honouring our agreement and let him go on the trip. When my husband called the scholar, he said his only question for our son was, 'Can you handle it?' He put the onus of the decision squarely on our son's shoulders. Thinking back, the scholar was wise beyond his years. These four words said so much to a young adult. The weightiest message in these words was that he acknowledged and respected our son as one capable of making decisions for himself, and that he was also fully aware of the consequences of his decision. The bottom line was, he was not choosing to do what was prohibited. In that case, whatever his decision was, it was of lesser importance. The problem was that his father and I were still stuck in the habit of making decisions for a young man who was nearly eighteen years old! It took me years to grasp this unforgettable experience to learn the importance of letting go as a parent.

Be a Means to Your Children's Wellbeing

Two key things you do to enhance their wellbeing are quality time you spend with them and your dua (prayers) for them.

Quality Time. Children crave their parents' attention. Young children are more forward in showing this need than older children. Busy parents who have to juggle their career and raise their children find it hard to make time to spend with their children. Even if they are at home, they are busy catching up on chores around the house. I can only empathise what their energy reserves look like! Try to schedule your quality time with your children. Make it a priority. I say this with earnest urgency. Do not wait until it is too late.

The key to quality time is being emotionally and psychologically present with your child. It does not matter what you do, as long as you do it together. Play a game with them. Bake, cook, clean, run around in the park, sing, draw, or fix a broken pipe... whatever the activity, make sure you are both engaged and emotionally present for each other. The quality time you spend with your children is a worthy investment in enhancing your and your children's wellbeing.

Pray For Them (Dua). Parents' prayers for their children are God's treasures on tap. It is readily accessible to anyone at any time under any circumstance. There will be times when you cannot be with your children. You will be tested to the end of your tethers. When you feel you have come to a dead end and there is nothing you can do to help your children, you are wrong. This is a time when you actively kneel and stretch out your hands to God for help. He is All-Hearing and All-Knowing. He will never forsake you. Dip into this treasure chest often. Follow the example of Prophet Ibrahim (peace be upon him) who prayed for his offspring, for their guidance, leadership, security and provision[145] from which the dwellers of Makkah are still reaping the benefit to this day.

Conclusion

This chapter explores the concept of external encounters that include creations and experiences, which I call external encounters collectively. External/Outward

Connection is an opportunity to enhance our wellbeing. The more difficulties we overcome through the external encounters the more tools we have to move forward in life. A considerable part of this discussion was dedicated to viewing children as an external encounter and how parents can connect with them to enhance their wellbeing. They are also a means for us to close the loop for our own wellbeing. Of the many external connections we make in our lives, our connections with our children are also amongst the most rewarding.

CHAPTER NINE
Applying The 1-2-3 Wellbeing Guide

Try telling someone about your experience, a meaningful one... but you are dismissed, or others switch off. It is only when the time and place are right that it all clicks. Therefore, never stop trying, for you shall knock and the door will be opened.[146]

IN THE PREVIOUS chapters I have discussed at length each component of the proposed 1-2-3 Parent Wellbeing Guide. How do we put it into practice? How do we translate understanding into action? More importantly, how do we know if our practice has really served our wellbeing?

It has been recorded that three companions of the Prophet (may God be pleased with them) fought side by side in one of the battles. When people brought water to one of them, one saw his companion looking at the water. So he told the person to take the water to him first. When water was brought to the second person, he told the person to give water to the third. By the time water was brought to the third companion, others found the first two had breathed their last. Their level of faith is legendary.[147] It is hard for me as an ordinary person to fathom how at that dire moment they could implement the principle behind the Hadith that says 'none of you (truly) believes until he wishes for his brother what he wishes for himself.'[148] It seems that their focus on the eternal blessing had taken root in their hearts so firmly that their screaming physical discomfort could be effectively silenced. What was it like?

The extent of connection in these companions was at another level. Nevertheless, we have our tests and battles customised for us that befit our capabilities, no more, no less. This reminds me of a body pump class I attended some years ago. I wondered how the instructor could do it with such ease lifting her twenty-kilogram weights. But as a beginner one kilogram was all I could handle and that would have to be good enough. I slowly built to one and half then onto two kilograms after a term of persistent practice at the gym. Although we can never compare our encounters to those giants whom we take as our role models, we can still strive to build our character starting with our own encounters within our own contexts in our own capacity. We can and we should, in our own way strive to attain the highest level of peace in our heart. It matters not from which point we start. We just need to start.

Attaining ultimate wellbeing is an ongoing process. It is a destination that one continuously strives to arrive at.

Every experience and lesson learnt adds more depth to the construct.

Scientists in the field of positive psychology are designing measurable ways to prove how different elements of wellbeing can be achieved. Their tools consist of brain scans, questionnaires and surveys, among others, where participants are asked to score their subjective wellbeing. Peace and tranquillity of the heart is subjective and intangible. It is for you to notice how you arrived at a particular decision and assess how at peace you feel after each conscious decision you made at each crossroad. If the intention plus action (good deed) in hindsight leave you with contentment and no regret, then you are likely to have nurtured your own wellbeing by a fraction. My advice to myself and all of my readers is to keep collecting those tiny jewels of contentment. Even at times when you falter, having the right mindset means you are at liberty to choose how you see the situation and how you can amend it. Make it a positive addition to your experience.

This chapter presents a number of life examples to demonstrate how the 1-2-3 Wellbeing Guide can be applied. The sweetness of a tranquil heart as a result of striving consistently in pursuit of the Creator's pleasure is the ultimate wellbeing to which I refer repeatedly in this book. The Guide provides an easy-to-remember formula to strive for the true satisfaction within. It takes us deeper than the pleasures of receiving tangible rewards. It is that wholesome feeling in our hearts that contributes to our ultimate wellbeing.

To start with, I would like to reflect on a few personal experiences along this journey. I will also introduce the APCAR (acronym for Aware-Ponder-Connect-Act-Review) process to help you implement the 1-2-3 Wellbeing Guide.

Personal Experiences

In teaching, we were trained to use a number of different approaches to help students learn a concept. Most times we show students what to do. Other times we bring them contrasts to let them see what not to do. To demonstrate what it is like to not having the Wellbeing Guide in place, allow me to share one of my many blunders with you. I will also introduce and explain the APCAR process to help you enhance your wellbeing.

The Prayer Mat

It was in the first year after I got married. At the time we lived in Saudi Arabia. My husband and I were at a marketplace when the athan (call) for Maghrib prayer (just after sunset) came in. The hustle and bustle in the market stopped. My husband went to join the makeshift congregation with the men. While I waited in the car, I noticed a lady by the roadside selling small packets of roasted chickpeas. She took out her prayer mat. My eyes were immediately drawn to her thin blue mat, worn out and discoloured.

I suddenly had a thought to give her the prayer mat in the back of our car. But I was tangled up by my own conflicting thoughts and I could not decide what to do. My mother's voice said: 'I treasure my worn-out prayer mat more than any other.' My mind went to the Hadith that said a good woman should 'guard her husband's property in his absence.' Being newly married and scared to make mistakes, I did not know if I needed permission to give away my husband's prayer mat.

I later realised that not making a decision was a decision in itself. When I disclosed my internal conflict with my husband much later on, he wished he could turn back the clock for me to carry out my initial intention. That was over thirty years ago and to this day I regret not listening to my heart.

Analysis of the Blunder

Using the 1-2-3 Wellbeing Guide to analyse that incident, I can see the blockages that interfered with the flow of my encounters, namely my thoughts and decisions. In that incident I had no concept of closing the loop to attaining wellbeing. Knowing what I know now, I can clearly see how things could have turned out differently had I applied the 1-2-3 Wellbeing Guide.

Knowledge

In my case, the knowledge was of two levels. Firstly, the saying that 'a little knowledge can be a dangerous thing' can be applied to my lack of understanding of how holistically a Hadith should be applied. Taking a speck of knowledge without understanding the context or essence behind it can become a stumbling block to doing what is more appropriate. I am thankful for having been guided to where I am today, that is, knowing there is still so much more I am yet to learn. Secondly, back then I needed time to get to know the person I was married to. My over-cautiousness prevented me from doing what came to me spontaneously, but through that incident my husband's character was revealed to me. His reaction gave me the confidence to act on a good intent in the days and years that followed. That was a time when I was only beginning to learn about my role as a young wife, as I was learning about my purpose in life.

Inward Connection

I was not strongly connected to my inner self. I did not trust my own instinct. Had I honoured and captured that initial spark, I could very easily have disputed my analytic mind. To my mother's voice I could have argued with myself—giving the lady another prayer mat was not equal to devaluing her old one, that is *if* she had the same sentiments to treasure her old mat as my mum. Giving away the mat was not equal to failing to guard my husband's property either. Quite the contrary. The meaning of safeguarding has two folds. When I think about what is kept, it can be a keeping for this transient life or a keeping for the eternal life. Had I known the Two-Fold concept, the voices of my mother and from my readings would have become floating references that arose on the horizon without becoming the determining factors for my choice in that moment between my Double-Selection.

Vertical Connection

My analytic mind overruled my vertical connection. When the prayer mat caught my eyes and pulled on my heartstrings, I let my analytical mind take the driver's seat. That analytical mind was arguably also striving for vertical connection, in a less than persuasive manner.

One-Way Journey Home

I did not apply the one-way journey home concept through my action. I had not thought that sometimes, an opportunity to do good, once missed, is gone forever. To close the loop for ultimate wellbeing, I must wear the hat of a scavenger for opportunities and snap it up the moment it shows its face at me. I did not know that our prayer mat could have earned all of us rewards each time the lady prayed on it without reducing any rewards she would receive from our Generous Lord. I must never underestimate the impact of a random act of kindness on my wellbeing.

I have had many more occasions when my analytical mind and over-cautiousness got in my way of spontaneous intents to do something good. The above and many other incidents often left me feeling regretful. As I work on connecting inwardly, I begin to accept myself, my wins and my losses. The incidents that used to leave me with regrets have become my motivation to do better. They became the reasons for my growth. My growth has been slow but I tell myself slow growth is better than no growth at all. I am not in any race with anyone. Those experiences are as precious as incidents where I walked away feeling content and peaceful.

The APCAR Process

Reflecting on events in hindsight is helpful but not constructive unless one starts to take concrete action. I wish to suggest a simple process to implement the 1-2-3 Wellbeing Guide when you need to take action. As stated above, this process is called APCAR, acronym for Aware-Ponder-Connect-Act-Review.

Aware

Know what is happening. Listen to your heart. Pay attention to that spur of the moment thought. This is your Inward Connection upon encountering a stimulus. Voices or thoughts that come immediately after can be from your inciting nafs, the analytics of your mind, social expectations, or God forbid, whisperings of the devil.

Ponder

Process the analytics that tell you otherwise. Do not bundle them up as distractions. They can be voices of caution that are there to protect you. Challenge those thoughts. Ask yourself: 'If I listened to these voices, will my action (or inaction) be more pleasing to my Creator?' This is where you apply the 'Two-Fold' process.

Connect Vertically

Ask God to guide your heart and action (Vertical Connection). Apply the 'Double-Selection' process to make a decision. Align what your heart desires against what is more pleasing to God. Consider which decision gives you the best of both worlds. Decide which way you are better able to live with your conscience.

Act/Rectify

Act on your decision. This is where you connect externally. This is what you have decided to pack into your 'bag' for your journey home. In some cases, you might want to rectify an initial response.

Review

Check with your heart again afterwards when you can reflect, revise and improve.

Practising my own Wellbeing Guide has helped me learn a great deal about myself. My biggest problem is that I either think with my emotions, or I analyse the situation excessively. Either way does not serve me well. I am now able to recognise when I am emotional and withhold my decisions until I allow time to deal with my emotions. I am becoming more self-aware to catch myself from analysing out of habit, to purposefully turning inwardly to connect with my inner self, connecting vertically to check my intention and seeking guidance, then taking due action to connect externally to attain ultimate wellbeing.

APCAR On Training Wheels

I will now share with you two examples of me putting this APCAR process into practice. Upon reflection I know I obviously need more practice with my own Wellbeing Guide because I tripped up in both encounters, but I nevertheless walked away feeling more peaceful by rectifying my initial decision in time using the APCAR process.

The Bed Swap

In September 2016 I was blessed with the opportunity to perform Hajj for the third time. This time I went with a heightened awareness to guard against my inciting nafs and the whisperings of the Satan. I desperately wanted to do better than the previous times. I know my own weakness so I vigilantly watched out for potholes that may trip me up. I watched my tongue. I did not engage in idle talk. I reminded myself to withhold complaint, to accept anything that comes and to say Alhamdulillah (all praises are due to God). I said to my inciting self, 'Huh! I know all about your tricks and I have come prepared!' Right there and then I tripped. Without any warning, the tests hit me from the left field. There were two incidents.

The first one happened in Mina. Mina is a valley six kilometres to the east of Makkah. It is also known as the Tent City due to over three million pilgrims who set up camp here during Hajj each year. Pilgrims stop here the night before they travel to Mount Arafat—for staying on Mount Arafat is an essential ritual of Hajj. Due to the sheer number of people to be transported between Makkah and Mina, the six kilometres can take hours to travel by bus. A few of us decided to walk from our hotel in Makkah to our tents in Mina. As expected, we got to Mina before the bus arrived. I was the first to enter my allocated tent and genuinely felt grateful for the tightly spaced but clean and comfortable sleeping arrangements to be shared by twenty women. My bed number was eighteen, two beds away from the entrance. I made my bed and settled into my space.

When the bus arrived, one by one the sisters in my tent found their allocated spots. The sister who was given bed number twenty looked unimpressed, even slightly devastated. She asked me if there was any possibility anyone would swap beds with her. I kept silent. Then she directly asked if I would be willing to swap with her.

Can you believe I said 'no'? In that very moment I caught myself, and immediately regretted it (*Awareness*). I paused and thought (*Ponder*) to myself—it should make no difference to me whether I was by the door or two steps from the door. What would be more pleasing to God? (*Two-Fold*). Allah loves the good doers (*Connect Vertically*). If I declined a request of which I had the capacity to fulfill, I may never have this opportunity again (*One-Way Journey Home*), so I should do what she asked (*Double-Selection*). So just as quickly, I got up to gather my things and said to her 'Let's swap, I don't mind!' (*Act/Rectify*). I was and still am grateful that in that split second, Allah pulled me back in time, from falling off the cliff into a hole of regret (*Review*) during Hajj of all times! I found out later that this sister had a phobia of lizards!

The Massage

The second incident happened on the day of Arafat, the next day following the tent incident. Mount Arafat is situated twenty kilometres southeast of Makkah. All pilgrims must spend their day on this mountain until later in the afternoon. Each year three to four million people spend that day on that mountain in the intense heat seeking forgiveness and blessings from God. We were packed into a huge tent shared by over 500 women. Despite the large air-conditioning units labouring to help reduce the intensity of 50 plus degrees Centigrade in the hottest part of the day, we were still tested with some level of discomfort. Like everyone else I tried to concentrate on making the most of that blessed day amidst the heat and humidity. A lady sitting across from me started gesturing to me. Eventually I figured out that she wanted me to give her a head and shoulder massage. My immediate thought was that I wanted to benefit every second of this precious afternoon from dhikrullah (remembrance of God), so I said 'no', *again!*

To be honest, for a second I was slightly annoyed by her interruption. I wondered why of all people she picked me for this job. A wee voice asked (Satan teaming up with my inciting nafs): is it because you are the only Asian in the vicinity that she thinks you should serve her? Then my reproaching nafs started to scold me for not thinking well of this lady (*Awareness*). I paused and thought about this (*Ponder*). I challenged my nafs and my analytic mind: What is the objective of uttering words of (dhikrullah) remembrance of God (*Two-Fold*)? Isn't it to praise and to seek Allah's pleasure? But there are a thousand ways to achieve that; dhikrullah was only one of them. I heard myself asking, 'Do you realise you just turned down a sister's request to relieve her of a headache on the day of Arafat, the best day created for the entire year?' (*One-Way Journey Home, Connect Vertically*). I crushed the wee voice that came from my faint victim mentality surfaced from my subconscious (*Double-Selection*). I told myself, 'Whatever goes through this lady's mind is of no concern to you. You are only responsible for your intention and your own action. Close the loop while you can!' I supplicated, 'Ya Allah forgive me! Let me help this sister in whichever way I can. I don't want to live to regret it!'

All these thoughts went through my heart and mind in a matter of seconds. I got up and went over to her and said I would give it a try (*Act/Rectify*). In my heart I asked for forgiveness from my Merciful Lord. I used my fingers to redeem myself for my hesitation, for my victim mentality. I worked on her neck, her head, her shoulders and upper back. Gradually a smile came to her face. She looked relaxed and seemed to have enjoyed my untrained service. All it took was twenty minutes.

I aligned my connection three-ways (*Review*). I asked Allah to accept my repentance, on the best day of the year, right there at Arafat. I hope I passed my tests even though I was wobbly.

If my evaluation of my subjective wellbeing is anything to go by, I can honestly say I attained peace of heart from both incidents. Had I not rectified from my initial reactions I would have kicked myself possibly for the rest of my life.

Upon reviewing these two incidents after some time

had passed, I noticed a pattern in my reactions when external encounters came knocking on my door.

I notice I have a habit of saying 'no'. I know saying 'no' protects me most of the time, but saying 'no' can also make me lose golden opportunities to do good, with repercussions on my ultimate wellbeing. I am a typical example where Satan uses my caution against me by getting my mind to conjure up all kinds of reasons why I should not do a good deed. Unlike people who are charitable like the swift wind, I often have to go through internal wars with my nafs and my over-protective 'reasoning'. I recognise that I have much work to do. I want to be able to say 'no' because I have a burning 'yes' behind. More than this, I want to stop saying 'no' for no good reason. I want to say 'yes' more readily so I can be brought closer to my Lord. The place from which my decision comes has to be from a sound heart, and I cannot let it be pulled by either my analytical mind or my nafs. The positive side to this is, I now have better awareness of myself, I am on my way to establish habits to connect three ways, not for anyone else but for pleasing my Lord, to attain my own ultimate peace and wellbeing.

I suspect I am not the last person who goes through these internal struggles with the mind and nafs. I would even say these struggles are common unless people intentionally train themselves to connect in three ways with the goal of ultimate wellbeing in mind. Maybe some of you have experienced similar debates within yourselves. I urge you to adopt the APCAR process and experience the sweetness of living with yourself in peace.

Indeed, one would observe that whatever happens, happens only by the Will of God. Our internal struggles are our tests. Whenever you find yourselves at a crossroads desiring to do something you know in your heart is right, challenge your thoughts, go ahead with your intuition and do not look back. Turn your heart towards God, follow the path of the prophets, you cannot go wrong. You may still decide to stay with your decision to decline, but this time the decision is one that is well thought through so your heart is left with no regrets in hindsight. You may even notice signs over time that indicate to you whether you had made the right decision. Even if you realise that you could perhaps have chosen a different path, let that be a building block to grow, make it your motivation to do better in future.

There is no question that the key to doing what is right is by being totally honest with yourself no matter how bad you think you look. This is Inward Connection. Nothing can be more destructive than self-deception. Nothing can be more miserable than self-loathing. It takes tremendous courage to face your own weaknesses but it is the prerequisite for growth. Once you get past that fragile ego of yours and face yourself truthfully, you are on the road to better wellbeing.

Vertical Connection begins with seeking the correct knowledge of God. Let us take the well-known example of one companion of the Prophet who internalised his understanding of his Lord. Umar Ibn al-Khattab (may God be pleased with him) lived by the principle of holding himself accountable before he was held to account by God. He would patrol the streets of Madinah at night to seek out families who might be in need of his support. He even extended this mercy by checking the safety of the roads for fear that some animals might trip over holes in their paths.

He fulfilled his duty as the Caliph not from a place of dominance but from a mindful awareness of his accountability to God. His sincere intention to serve and his actions were what he chose to pack into his 'bag' for his journey home.

I wish to remind my readers that the examples of the great personalities in our history are there to motivate us. They have set the bar very high for those that came after them but they are never meant to make us feel unworthy. Just because we are lay Muslims does not mean our trials and challenges are any less worthy. Life lends us plenty of opportunities to implement the proposed Wellbeing Guide. We are constantly making decisions. A decision can be simple if the choice is between halal and haram. Life is never that simple. Many a time we are put in situations where we have to make difficult decisions suited to our level of knowledge and circumstances.

Applying The 1-2-3 Wellbeing Guide To Real Life Examples

Allow me to share a few more lived experiences in our time to help you familiarise with my Wellbeing Guide's application. The key characters in the following true stories may or may not have thought about their own experiences in light of my Wellbeing Guide. I am presenting their stories for my readers to interpret the elements through the 1-2-3 Wellbeing Guide that I believe to have helped them attain wellbeing. More importantly, I want my readers to pay attention to how they closed the loop for wellbeing through their external connections.

Calamity

On 26 January 1949 an overloaded steamer by the name of Taiping left Shanghai headed towards Keelung in Taiwan. Disaster struck after it collided with another smaller vessel. The steamer sank. Upon investigation, it was carrying some 1500 refugees fleeing the advancing Chinese Communist regime in Mainland China. It was overcrowded with more than double her capacity (rated to carry 580 passengers).

On board the steamer was my uncle, my father's eldest brother. He was the last of the family to leave China. My grandfather had entrusted my uncle to wrap up his business ventures and bring the bulk of his wealth for the large family's settlement in Taiwan. In that night, the fate of my family took an unexpected turn!

By the time I was born my grandfather was already in his seventies. He dedicated the last years of his life as a caretaker in Taipei Grand Mosque. My memory of him was a picture of serenity. I can still see the broad smile on his face when I sent him food at the mosque. I can still feel the warmth of his large soft hands when he put fifty cents into my hand to buy peanuts to munch on my way home. I kept the calligraphy brush he bought me to encourage me to keep practising my writing.

Today I am left to wonder—how did my grandfather come to terms with this heavy blow? I was told that he accepted like a true servant of God in full submission.

Somehow he found peace within himself over the tragic events.

The loss of my uncle meant that my father had to step up to shoulder most of the responsibilities as my grandfather's second son to help raise his younger siblings, support my uncle's widow and two young children, as well as finding ways to make ends meet in raising the growing number of children of his own.

As I got older I learnt to be thankful for God's far-reaching mercy. This could have been a blessing in disguise that saved us from the test of wealth when almost everyone on the small Taiwanese island faced multiple forms of hardship after the civil war between the Communist and the Nationalist parties.

My grandfather set an example for us to draw strength from faith to endure the double blow of losing his son and all his wealth. He obviously saw through the temporary life we are in and cast his vision on the one-way journey home. At the deepest of his sorrows, he never once turned to alcohol or gambling as both are prohibited in Islam. For his retirement he made the decision to offer his service to God. I was among the external connections he made with love and care. I pray that he is resting in peace and will journey on to Paradise in the Hereafter, where his beloved son, and all his loved ones, including me, will be with him forever.

Custody

The second example I wish to present here is the story of a late Islamic worker in North America, Aminah Assilmi (may Allah have mercy on her soul).

Aminah's conversion to Islam gave her peace spiritually yet she was trialled in great severity financially, physically and most of all, with her children. Almost all of her family broke away from her after she embraced Islam. The hardest test she had to encounter above all was fighting for custody of her children. This was back in the 1970s. She was in an impossible dilemma. The judge made her choose between her faith and her children. She mustered all possible strength within her to choose to hold on to the rope of God by a thread. What a grip that was! Sr Aminah Assilmi's Double-Selection was impossible to most!

Over the years Aminah continued to educate herself about Islam and became an active community leader and speaker on various topics in Islam. From initially wanting to kill her and admitting her into a mental institute, her family began to accept her over time. They not only accepted her choice, many of them accepted Islam through her. She had no knowledge that this honourable position was in store for her at the time she was given the ultimatum. Her decision to choose God over the worldly attachments opened the gate to such unexpected blessings!

Aminah remained active despite financial hardship and physical ailments. She died in a car accident on 5 March 2010 on her way home from a speaking engagement. May Allah grant her martyrdom (one who sacrificed her life in the path of her Lord). Her travel companion survived. He was none other than her own son. May

Allah let Sister Aminah rest in peace and accept all her struggles and sacrifices.

If you were to examine Aminah's major decisions from this story, it would not be difficult to see how the 1-2-3 Wellbeing Guide can be applied.

Total Submission

The third story is about Nadia whom I met on one of my travels. It was an evening in 2013 when my travel companion and I followed a scholar to visit a bereaved family. A young boy of about eight years old by the name of Yusuf came out of the kitchen to greet everyone. As he went around the big circle of women shaking hands with them, I noticed a lag in his gait and a scar on the back of his head. His mother, Nadia, was the grieving family's neighbour who came to help out. She came out of the kitchen when she had a minute to spare. She took the empty seat next to me.

We introduced ourselves and after some small talk, I inquired about her son. She beamed. She told me that Yusuf was her miracle child. When she was seven months pregnant the doctor strongly suggested abortion as she had detected hydrocephaly in her foetus. Hydrocephaly is a condition where fluids in the brain get accumulated inside the membranes that protect the brain, thus constricting the development and functioning of the brain. Surgical procedures may or may not succeed in draining the fluid away. Nadia's doctor warned that this child was at high risk of severe brain damage and multiple disabilities. The strain and challenges on the family were imminent. However, Nadia and her husband refused abortion and prepared themselves to accept whatever was decreed for them.

Over the years Yusuf underwent numerous surgical interventions to drain the fluid from his brain. We witnessed how well Yusuf communicated and he was mobile. Despite his global delay in development, Yusuf was found to have a special gift in reciting and memorising the Qur'an. He enjoyed school and could not be happier. From the light on Nadia's face I could tell that she had been rewarded beyond her wildest dreams. In those few minutes I must have heard Nadia saying 'Shukur' (grateful) more than twenty times! Yusuf's doctor was astounded by his progress.

Can you see how the 1-2-3 Wellbeing Guide at play that led to Nadia and her husband's decision to keep their child? Their vertical connection was strong and they did not have to wait long to see how their decision had closed the loop for wellbeing in this life. What could be waiting for Nadia and her husband in the Hereafter from the Generous Lord?

Terminal Illness

On 29 May 2018, the world mourned over the loss of 'one of the most remarkable humanitarians of its time'.[149] Born on 16 Feb 1982, Ali Banat was a young, successful Australian businessman who lived a lavish life in Greenacre, a suburb southwest of Sydney. Among his prized possessions were rows of Louis Vuitton shoes in his dressing room and a Ferrari Spider in his garage.

All this changed overnight. With no prior warning Ali was diagnosed with stage four mouth cancer in early 2015. Cancer had already spread through his bloodstream. He was told he only had seven months to live. Ali recalled in that moment the only thing he could say was 'Truly, we belong to Allah, and it is to Him that we shall return'. It was a defining moment when the penny dropped for Ali. He considered this illness as a 'gift' from his Lord because he saw it 'as a chance to change'. Ali gave away his expensive clothes and sold all his valuable possessions. In an interview on One Path, Ali expressed his desire to get rid of his worldly possessions.[150] In October 2015, Ali launched Muslims Around the World project and began his charity work to help people in need. Since then, projects to assist vulnerable people in the poorest of conditions in Africa, Lebanon and Bangladesh began to take off with much support from local and global communities. Although Ali is no longer with us, he left behind a legacy. The momentum he gathered for his projects continues to thrive today.

This is another person's example of managing life challenges. You may want to imagine how one can come to these decisions using the 1-2-3 Wellbeing Guide.

Forgiveness

The final story is about a man's decision in dealing with a heinous crime hurled at him that almost claimed his life. 'What would you do if you were shot in the face and left for dead?'[151] This was the opening sentence of Rais Bhuiyan's talk about the incident that shattered his life ten days after 9/11. Within seconds of the gunshot Rais' American dream turned into shards of an unthinkable nightmare.

Rais Bhuiyan had just arrived in America a few months prior to the incident. Nothing could have prepared Rais for what happened to him that night when he turned up for work at the petrol station. The man who pulled the trigger at him knew nothing about Rais. He was a white supremacist out to avenge the loss of Americans of the 9/11 tragedy. Rais was a victim of hate crime. Miraculously he survived. Piece by piece he spent the subsequent years to put his life back together—managed to finish his education, became an IT system manager and got married.

This was not all. What was truly remarkable about Rais was that he spent years fighting for Mark Stroman, the man who shattered his face and dreams, to be spared from execution. Why would anyone do that? 'Execution was not the solution,' Rais said. 'It would not eradicate hate crimes in this world. I had to save his life to make a change.'[152]

Just how did Rais deal with what happened to him? He had three dozen shotgun pellets left in his face. He lost one eye, his job, his home and his fiancé. 'It's like a scar,' he said. 'It may never go away. But you have the power to look at it and say, "I was able to heal it and get myself back."' He had every right to be angry and to seek revenge. Instead, he turned his energy into something much bigger, much more constructive, with greater purpose. He founded the World Without Hate, a not-for-profit organisation aimed at advocating and teaching the power of forgiveness and mercy.

The type of trials in the above stories are all different. They were nevertheless trials, very tough trials that some people had to face in life. None would have willingly chosen to be in any of those situations. Like my grandfather, no one could foresee what would unfold at the time they were hit with those blows. Yet each key character in their own ways demonstrated courage in submitting to what was decreed for them. They took it on, chose an option that aligned themselves with the will of the Creator at the crux of decision making, in return for their peace of heart. In a nutshell, these are examples of real people who were so connected internally and vertically, that made them decide to connect externally, to close the loop for their ultimate wellbeing in this life and more importantly, in the Hereafter.

What amazes me about these people is their courage to take the road less travelled because they saw the potential of living for a higher purpose. The worldly life is filled with things we love. We all get attached to something/someone at one stage or another… be it people, possession, lifestyle, wealth and even life itself. When we are being tested with losing them we naturally experience human emotions. Some of us allow our emotions to boil over, some find the strength within to deal with the ordeal. This does not mean they experienced less pain, anxiety, sadness, shock, disappointment, anger etc. However, these people demonstrated their ability to examine what lies underneath—they looked at the second fold then chose their response (Double-Selection). I believe all the central characters in the stories above had the 'one-way journey home' in mind. They must have carefully considered every step they took to make sure each step they took was aimed at getting closer to their final destination with a peaceful heart.

CHAPTER TEN

Go The Extra Mile

Patience is to faith what the head is to the body. Faith is of two halves, one is patience and the other is gratitude. Patience frees you from the shackles of calamity, and, prayer is one of the best means to attain spiritual growth, happiness and inner strength[153]

IN THIS BOOK I have proposed a simple guide to put the ultimate wellbeing in perspective. Positivity begets positivity. A grounded, calm, humble and productive parent stands a better chance of raising children who are grounded, calm, humble and productive. Both parents as the co-captains have a critical role to steer the ship with a clear destination in mind. During rough times you know you cannot stop the storm, but you can hold the wheel with steady hands to weather the crushing waves. Your understanding of what really matters and your regular practice becomes the lifejacket that keeps you calm in order to steer your crew to safety.

One virtue that I have deliberately left to discuss at the end is patience. This is because patience is among the most important virtues for parents. I will also share a first aid measure with the acronym BRAT when your children push your button.

Patience (Sabr)

The Arabic word for patience is Sabr. Sometimes the same word can be translated as steadfastness or perseverance. If one hopes to be successful, let him be patient. God says in the Qur'an, 'You who believe, be steadfast, more steadfast than others; be ready; always be mindful of God, so that you may prosper.'[154] Among the best of blessings is the ability to be patient.

In the Qur'an, Luqman advised his son to live by the same aspirations as mentioned in the previous verse. He said, 'Keep up the prayer, my son; command what is right; forbid what is wrong; bear anything that happens to you steadfastly: these are things to be aspired to.'[155]

Some people may attribute patience to one's temperament. We can see it in young children where one may demonstrate more patience than others. While I am not going to dispute there exists differences in our natural temperaments, I certainly believe that patience is not an exclusive ability that only certain people are gifted with. It is something that one can attain and reap its benefit by putting in effort over time. Are some children naturally more patient or is it because they feel more secure, are more trusting and better skilled in solving problems? According to Gottman, children who receive emotion coaching from their parents demonstrate better emotional intelligence.[156] This means they are better equipped with tools to deal with difficulties. Instead of being caught up in emotions, they channel their energy to deal with the situation. It is productive patience. Productive patience can be cultivated by parents.

As adults we may have missed the chance to be emotion coached by our parents when we were children, we still have hope. We are given plenty of situations in life that force us to learn this virtue. Our children are in a way sent to us to grow our patience. Ibn Qayyim writes about the three situations when one needs to be patient. These are: patience in doing good deeds, patience in staying away from sins, and patience in surrendering to God's decree and destiny.[157] The following section discusses these three situations.

Patience In Doing Good Deeds

If you wonder why we need to be patient in doing good deeds, let me remind you of a well-known story. There was a man who, on the morning after his wedding, fought hard to go to the mosque to perform his morning prayer at the first break of dawn. It is hard for anyone to leave the warm and cosy bed at 4am at the best of times. One can imagine what a struggle it would have been for a newly married man. He overcame his own nafs and headed towards the mosque. A gust of wind blew out his light. He persisted. He lit his candle and walked on. Some distance later, another gust of wind blew out his light the second time. He persisted until the third time, when the devil appeared to light the path for him. The devil said to the man, 'I give up. My effort in pulling you the other way only caused you to earn more reward. I can't bear to watch you accumulate reward anymore! I thought I better hurry you along instead!'

What can you take from this story? For me, the message is written in bold as: DO NOT BE DETERRED BY SETBACKS WHEN YOU INTEND TO DO WHAT IS RIGHT! This is because while the devil wants the nafs to indulge in sins, he also cannot bear to see one who insists on doing what is right.

Once my husband was delivering a huge table in the back of his station wagon to a family in need. He had to turn extra slowly at a set of traffic lights due to a third of the table hanging low from the back of his car. While he cautiously made the turn the lights changed from green to orange to red and he got flashed. He was fined $180 and lost two demerit points while that table only cost him $10 to buy! A tow truck would have charged a similar price minus the demerit points. I clearly remember him shaking his head as he explained to me what happened that night saying, 'You have to be patient even when you try to do a good deed!'

How would you interpret such experiences? Would you consider these obstacles as tests on your sincerity and patience? Or would you throw the towel in? The devil made his pledge that he would wait for the believers along their paths to lead them astray, so that he would not have to dwell in Hell alone. Rewards are earned. We need to work for them. Some rewards are earned through sacrifices. No prophets carried out their missions without encountering hardship. Nothing of value can be attained without effort.

If we remember this, it will help us to remain patient when faced with difficulties in our pursuit of a worthy cause.

Patience In Staying Away From Sins

God warned people on many occasions to not 'go near' certain sins such as adultery, unlawfully consuming an orphan's properties, etc. This is because our Creator knows our inclinations better than we know ourselves.

Being patient in staying away from sins requires one to find ways to keep the inciting nafs at bay. From glancing over the shoulder of the high achiever sitting next to you in a test, to telling a 'little lie' in order to get out of trouble, we know in our hearts that these are acts of disobedience. Even when we get away with it, we know we have done wrong. This is fitrah, a natural disposition in us like an inbuilt compass; in this case, an innate knowing that certain actions are wrong. Somehow, we are still tempted to commit these seemingly 'small' sins. This is because in our hasty nature, we want to find shortcuts to get what we want, or to avoid the unpleasant, at the expense of our souls. Little things grow into big things. Beware of the habits we develop over time.

Patience In Surrendering To God's Decree And Destinty

Among the hardest trials a person could encounter are trials related to one's children. How does one remain patient when such situations strike? Mental preparation is important. 'Your wealth and your children are only a test for you. There is great reward with God'.[158] Death, mental illness, disability, terminal illness, rebellion, risky behaviour, anti-social behaviour ... these are all forms of heartbreaking trials that are devastating to a person, let alone helplessly watching one's own children going through them.

Many years ago a dear friend of mine lost her 18-year-old son. This was a son of every mother's dreams. He was respectful, pious, and loving. Over the years I watched how this grief-stricken mother mourned her loss in dignity, acceptance and patience. I could see it was her Three-Way Connection that sustained her. She had a deep understanding that her son was taken to a better place. The pain was something that would never go away, she told me, you learn to manage it. She continued to keep herself busy with work and be the glue that held her large family together. She took the first opportunity to work overseas. Upon returning several years later she realised that the job overseas was what she needed at the time. She was 'sent' away to heal. This was one lady who was well connected in all three ways.

Sometimes there is no explanation but we may come to understand some of these trials in their right time. Prophet Nuh's (Noah, peace be upon him) effort to save his family and his people is well documented. In the Qur'an we learn that Prophet Nuh had to watch one of his son's own demise. Sometimes the only right thing to do as a parent is to submit to what has been decreed and trust that one day we will come to comprehend the hidden mercy behind the seemingly incomprehensible.

Understanding How To Be Patient

I have sat through many sermons and lectures on the virtues of patience, the different situations when patience was the most befitting, and stories of people who were patient. But my capacity to be patient did not really change until I was put through situations that gave me insight to what being patient entailed. I came to the conclusion that only through trials can one really appreciate the value of patience. This section is a summary of what makes sense to me about patience. I believe my understanding will always be a work in progress.

Being patient is a verb. To be patient involves purpose, restraint, action, acceptance and trust.

Purpose

As an adult, an understanding of why you need to be patient makes being patient worth enduring.

Most people intend to do good and want to do well at what they do. How often do people quit because of setbacks, boredom, hastiness, distractions, negative self-talks, laziness and so on? Patience in doing good deeds involves our ability to stay the course. Angela Duckworth, whose research focus has largely been on grit and perseverance observes, 'Enthusiasm is common. Endurance is rare'.[159] Without patience and a strong sense of purpose, even the most praiseworthy project can flop into a heap.

I have come to appreciate that true patience and ego cannot coexist. Impatience is a result of us letting our inciting nafs take charge to serve the lower desires or to *ensure* we get certain outcomes. These desires are like sparks which can flare into a raging fire if one does not actively stamp it out in time. One can be so caught up by these desires and hopes that one temporarily forgets Who is really in charge of all matters.

Restraint

This calls for a person's self-awareness in order to translate knowledge into action. Without activating the heart, knowledge concerning patience does not automatically lead to action. Being patient requires one to actively engage in self-restraint. It is a commitment that involves knowledge, mindfulness practice and deliberate, achievable actions.

Resilience, bounce back, delayed gratification and grit are some areas within Positive Psychology that are associated with success in life. All of these involve purpose, patience, and in particular, the will power to restrain. Examples include restrain from giving up, restrain from taking the easier way, restrain from avoiding the uncomfortable, restrain from anger and restrain from overindulgence.

Recognising that certain burning desires have ill consequences is the first step to restrain. If one follows this recognition with a plan to curb this desire, restraint starts to take shape. Like a tug-of-war, the heart needs to want the counterbalance more to restrain from pleasing the lower self.

Certain sins creep up on us quietly; sometimes our nafs and Satan team up to present a 'noble' justification in disguise. Therefore all deliberate measures to safeguard ourselves are necessary.

Action

I used to think being patient meant to do nothing except to quietly endure. Life taught me that this is not always the case. Granted, endurance is a part of being patient. There are some things one can actively engage in while one feels completely helpless. One can zoom out to refocus on the bigger picture, for example. One can actively take a step back and look beyond the immediate trial. By doing so one's situation often takes on a new perspective. Zooming out reminds us of why we are doing what we are doing. One can actively look for the mercy of God, or actively seek to purify oneself in asking for God's forgiveness for sins committed knowingly and unknowingly.

Another form of action is to actively close off the ports that temptations enter to ignite our lower desires. Our sensory organs are these ports of entry. This requires one to have a high level of self-awareness, and having the right knowledge helps. It could be the thought of gaining more power, wealth or fame through impermissible means. It could start off as a flicker of an indecent thought. Take pornography, for instance. Catholic Online writes, 'Online pornography is one of the fastest growing addictions in the United States on par with cocaine and gambling.'[160] Its effects on a person's behaviour have been strongly associated with violence and brutality.[161] The first port of entry for this sin is the sight. The image, once beheld, immediately contaminates the mind, and darkens the heart. Therefore never underestimate temptations to sin. Close off the ports of entry at one's first awareness.

Our minds are like a machine that constantly needs to be fed with materials to process. Once the ports of entry are guarded, you must keep busy in seeking beneficial knowledge and engaging in productive work that distance you from the luring tentacle of temptations that draws you toward the sin.

Surrender

To some this may seem fatalistic but for a believer acceptance is essential to one's wellbeing. It takes grit for one to persevere; it takes wisdom to know when to let go. Doctors treating terminally ill patients know when to recommend a patient for palliative care. Not every matter is within our jurisdiction to get an outcome we want. Certain things are not in our control. Acceptance is an internal act of submission. Accepting that hardship and pain are part and parcel of life strengthens our ability to be patient when our hearts are troubled.

As parents there are bound to be times when we question ourselves where we went wrong with our parenting decisions or approach. The first thing you need for your own wellbeing is to accept yourself, flaws and all. 'O you who believe, seek aid through patience and prayer. Allah indeed is with those who are patient.'[162] You, like most parents throughout history, are learning as you go. You can only do the best you know how. You have the capacity to learn and do things differently.

What does acceptance look like? It looks like a person who seeks to be still after whatever initial human reactions had taken place; a person who gives his entire being the chance to reset to that place of tranquillity; one who is tuning in to discover the message from beyond. Acceptance during trying times means one remembers to be thankful that things could have but did not turn out ten times worse. It enables one to shift from a place of negativity to a place of gratitude and trust.

Trust

When things are hard, it is one's deep level of trust that keeps one afloat. Without trust, one easily loses hope. This trust deepens after one comes out from each difficult experience. These experiences on reflection add to one's faith in the greater plan that there is always something better in store, not if, but when the time is right. He trusts with a quiet calmness despite being shaken. To me, this is what patience encapsulates.

Trust helps a person to endure the anxiety associated with the unknown, to let things unravel in their due course, and to have faith that from the depth of pain and uncertainty things will turn out for the better. Sometimes you see God's mercy almost immediately, or soon after, other times much later, if not in this life, then definitely in the Hereafter. Examples of God's mercy can be found in the three incidences Prophet Musa had encountered with the man who was granted mercy and knowledge from God. Each incident illustrates God's blessings in the immediate, later in life, and reserved for one's offspring respectively.[163] These stories can be found in the 18th chapter in the Qur'an.

If along your journey of raising your child you face challenges over which you have absolutely no control, do not despair. Be hopeful that something better is in store for you, or be thankful that you have been saved from something worse. It is hard when it comes to our own flesh and blood. Being able to make the distinction between our effort and the outcome helps. Through our children's hardship there are lessons for them as well as for us if we observe and reflect; each person benefits from the challenges as intended, of which I call divine medicine. My children are all adults now. In hindsight I see that in trying to fulfill my role as a mother, what I needed was a paradigm shift when my children went through difficult times.

Over the years I began to notice the blessings embedded in life's ups and downs; especially the downs. Our Lord says in the Qur'an that He will test which of us are best in deeds.[164] It is in the pursuit we are being tested—our intention and our effort. This is where believing in our spiritual existence and why we live this worldly existence start to make sense.

This life is like a traveller passing through a port of transit. Life on earth is only a small segment of the whole journey. It is temporary. When you sit for a test, you will never think to live in that examination hall. You go in, you give it your best, and when the time is up, you leave. You sat the exam hoping to pass to qualify for something better. Likewise, our life on earth when viewed as a test, we want to live it well for something better in the Hereafter. While we are alive, we strive to pass our test for a better existence in the Hereafter. We strive to attain the ultimate wellbeing. The following subsection discusses how to grow patience like we grow our muscles. This will be followed by an introduction to BRAT (Breathe-Remember-Ask-Think Ihsan[165] [Ihsan means achieving mastery or excellence and the word also refers to sincerity in worship]) to help us deal with times when our patience are being tested.

Grow Your Muscles Of Patience

Patience is something we cannot have too much of. Children are the litmus test to our capacity to be patient. As God says, 'Your wealth and your children are only a test for you. There is great reward with God: be mindful of God as much as you can; hear and obey and give— it is for your own good.'[166] Remembering how you came through other difficulties in life increases your faith in the Most Merciful God at the most trying times. When you find yourself stuck in a dead end, leave the project to rest for some time but make sure you come back to it. Seeing the task with fresh eyes may mean that you notice things you missed before or that you are rested enough to continue with renewed energy.

How do we grow *muscles of patience*? The best answer is leave this up to our Lord who alone knows what we need. Do not ask for patience, rather ask for wellbeing. But when you are tested, it helps to remind yourself that you are going through 'growing pains'; that your Lord is giving you a growth spurt to grow your muscle of patience. This is because the only way to strengthen your endurance is by going through hardship. While we cannot will our *muscle of patience* to grow, the perspective through which we see our trials makes the process bearable.

One of the experiences that helped me grasp how hardship increases one's capacity to be patient was a skin infection I had to endure, not once but twice several decades ago.

The first time I had the infection I had no idea what it was. I noticed some pain in a spot on the back of my leg and dismissed it as a big pimple. I thought it would go away after a few days. Even though I normally have more tolerance for pain than the average person I know, that 'pimple'—on a scale of zero to ten—began with an intensity of a four that rapidly climbed to a nine within a couple of days. Those few days felt like weeks.

Being a person who likes a challenge, when the 'pimple' did not back off, I stubbornly decided to battle it out with my will instead of seeing a doctor. I was curious to see just how much pain a pimple could generate! I had difficulty walking. I could not pray properly. It kept me restless at night. I placed a doughnut made out a triangular bandage underneath the 'pimple' to avoid pressing on it directly. The radius of the swollen area kept expanding until I had to use two bandages to make a giant doughnut. I washed the swollen pimple with antiseptic and tried to keep the area clean and dry. I used ice packs to ease the pain. Then one day a volcano of pus and blood erupted from the site. Luckily this happened while I was at home. As much as I was caught off guard and annoyed by the mess, I was immensely grateful for the instant relief that came with it. The pain and swelling subsided over the next few days and eventually the ordeal was over.

Unfortunately, I was infected once again but the second time around I knew better what to expect. It was not less painful but my preparedness eased the anxiety and helped me cope better with the discomfort during the wait. I almost welcomed the pain when it cranked up its intensity because I knew then it would be an indication that it was nearing its eruption. It was then I knew my muscle of tolerance for this type of pain had expanded. Thankfully I never had another such infection since.

Thinking back, it was during a period of time when I

had a lot to deal with both physically and mentally that my immunity was compromised, which could have made me more susceptible to that particular type of skin infection.

I have come to the conclusion that certain pain in life happens to increase our capacity for other virtues. The pain was part of the process to rid my body of the infection. It was a cleansing process. Unless we have been put through the fire, we would not know what it entailed or appreciate our increased capacity to accept what was reserved for us. That was a test of my physical wellbeing.

We will surely be tested in many different areas throughout our life. I have learnt that patience during the darkest and hardest moment can only be achieved if we engage ourselves constantly in vertical connection. The break of dawn only comes after the darkest moment of the night. What followed from the endurance were the relief, gratitude, and that subtle sense of happiness for having come out at the other end more reassured, thankful, stronger, kinder and wiser. One comes to know one's potential to grow into something that one did not think one was capable of. Hardship avails you of the chance to transform into a better person. If similar trials happen again, you are the wiser for it, as you know what you need to do. This capacity to be patient can be transferred to other taxing situations. When other trials take place, you have been taught the meaning of trust which you otherwise would not have known.

In short, the trials help you unleash the potential for what you are meant to become. The more you are tested, the more tools you develop for coping with challenging situations. Trials avail a person the opportunity to 'grow' *muscles of patience*. Even if you cannot see your patient muscles grow, taking steps to keep your mind occupied during the seemingly 'endless' wait is what helps to make you develop patience. You are more likely to cope better during your future trials.

What about how to live by the Hadith that says 'patience is at the first stroke of a calamity'?[167] Well, for those of us who have children, we are given plenty of training opportunities to live by this Hadith. You may find the following tool helpful. I call it BRAT (acronym for Breathe, Remember, Ask and Think Ihsan), the first aid to testing moments.

Brat—First Aid During Testing Times

How do you keep calm in moments when your child presses your button? Practise **BRAT**, which is the acronym for Breathe-Remember-Ask-Think Ihsan.

Breathe

Take a deep breath. When our adrenalin puts us in fight or flight mode we tend to tense up, and hold our breath. Do not forget to breathe. Regulating your breath helps you to stay calm. Your brain needs oxygen. You need a truckload of calm during these crunch times.

Remember

Remember God does not burden a soul more than it can bear. You can do this. You may need help but you can do it. Reciting a prayer or Ayatul Kursi silently to yourself really helps. I have even noticed it not only calms me, it works on my child too!

Ask

Ask yourself: what is your child's reason for misbehaving? Attention seeking? Is she unwell, tired, or is she upset about something? It gives you a quick window to check the motive. If you go through a quick process of elimination and it seems that this child is pushing his/her boundaries to test your limits, then you need to decide quickly if this is a right time to take action. Assess your own mood and energy. Ask yourself if you are reacting to your own frustrations, or does the child's behaviour warrant your serious attention? It prevents you from acting out of reflex.

Think Ihsan (Highest God Consciousness)

This means to be mindful that your Examiner, the Almighty God, is watching you from above. What would be a best way to handle this? Draw strength from your Creator to guide you to manage the situation in a way that is fair to the child, and that gives you peace of mind.

For a prime example of what to do when a parent is pushed severely by his own children, let us remember Prophet Ya'qub's (Jacob, peace be upon him) ordeal. Upon hearing his older sons breaking the 'news' of Yusuf being killed by a wolf, this was how Prophet Ya'qub responded, 'No! Your souls have prompted you to do wrong! But it is best to be patient: from God alone I seek help to bear what you are saying!' Years later when again Prophet Ya'qub's older sons told him that Yusuf's younger brother Benjamin was kept behind in Egypt because he was caught stealing, he responded again with patience. He said, 'No! Your souls have prompted you to do wrong! But it is best to be patient: may God bring all of them back to me—He alone has the knowledge to decide…'[168]

Prophet Ya'qub (peace be upon him) did not blame or punish his children for that grave sin they committed. He identified it was his older children giving in to their inciting nafs that led them to their heinous act. This came from a father who was close to his children and knew his children well. He told his children that it was their nafs that influenced their decision to sin, indicating they had the ability to choose to do differently. He did not gloss over their wrongdoing but at the same time he put the potential power to change directly into the children's hands.

How did he deal with his worries and anger? He made a conscious decision to remain patient. Did he not experience sadness? He was so sad he lost his sight the second time he was struck with a test regarding his other son, Benjamin. That was the physical response of a father's intense sorrow. Yet he never lost sight of his Lord's mercy and infinite knowledge. He responded with restraint and hope.

Prophet Ya'qub's (peace be upon him) response is hard for the average parent to emulate. Remembering his test helps us gain better perspective of our own. A test is your customised training because your Examiner desires good for you and He knows what you can handle. For believers the perspective that 'No fatigue, nor disease, nor sorrow, nor sadness, nor hurt, nor distress befalls a Muslim, even if it were the prick he receives from a thorn, but that Allah expiates some of his sins for that'[169] offers a lot of comfort.

Not a leaf falls without the knowledge of the Creator of the universe.[170] It is all part of the greater plan. All the prophets have been through the hardest of trials. Olympians train hard and sacrifice much for a greater goal. Similarly, you are put through the process of hardship to be purified, and strengthened.

Reflecting on your past experiences helps you develop that sense of reassurance even when you are in the middle of a trial. Remember those times when you have come out of dire situations. How did you feel in hindsight? Remaining hopeful gives you the air to stay afloat during hard times.

Exercise your ability to self-regulate. When hardship hits, you have two options: react or respond. You can react by blowing up, or sit around and mope. Alternatively, you can respond by silently praying for guidance or doing something constructive to help you process the situation. You can allow yourself to vent, but put a cap on how long you do this. Tears cool the heart but excessive sadness leads to depression and hopelessness. Surround yourself with things and people who remind you of your Lord's mercy and love so you can reset your heart to a place of gratitude. Gratitude enhances positivity. Positivity broadens and builds.

Whatever you hope for may be great; know that what has been destined for you is greater. Patience is hard but not impossible. It is for our ultimate wellbeing that we strive; patience makes our striving meaningful.

Having discussed patience at length, I wish to bring your attention back to wellbeing because it is preferred for a believer to ask for wellbeing than to ask for patience to endure hardship. It was narrated that once the Prophet (peace and blessings be upon him) heard a man while he was saying: 'O Allah, indeed, I ask You for patience.' He said: 'You have asked Allah for trial, so ask Him for al-'Afiyah (wellbeing).'[171]

The merits for seeking wellbeing are further emphasised in the following Hadiths. Collected by at-Tirmidhi, the Prophet (peace and blessings be upon him) was reported to have said, 'Allah is not asked anything more beloved to Him than wellbeing.'[172] Anas ibn Malik reported: 'The Messenger of Allah, peace and blessings be upon him, said, "Ask your Lord for forgiveness and wellness in the world and the Hereafter. If you are given forgiveness and wellness in the world and the Hereafter, you have succeeded."'[173]

Concluding Words

In this humble endeavour I have assembled a guide for you to develop your wellbeing, not only as an investment for yourself, but also with the wellbeing of your children in mind. When we keep our entire existence in view, we see the bigger picture and our perspectives become clearer.

Remember we are on our One-Way Journey Home. Whatever hardship or pleasure, they are all temporary. We take them in our stride because we are going home. Every step we take on Earth is a step that brings us closer to home. Focusing on what we wish to pack into our 'bags' for our journey home is a sobering reminder to focus on what really matters.

Secondly, we use the Two-Fold thinking process to examine each encounter and ponder upon our Creator's greatness. Remember whatever happens to us, happens only by the will of God, the Lord of the universe. When it comes to deciding our course of actions, the Double-Selection process gives us the tool to look at our options and choose whatever is more worth packing into our 'bags' that will help us attain a tranquil heart.

Our human-ness means that our heart does not stay in the same status all the time. For this heart to know and desire that peaceful state, it needs regular maintenance. Which brings us to the third element of the Wellbeing Guide.

Connect Inwardly. Accept and celebrate your human-ness. Try to understand 'yourself' with honesty. Examine your emotion iceberg. Seek to understand the layers of constructions and narratives that led you to where you are now. Examine yourself objectively and be kind to yourself.

Connect Vertically. Be grateful for the knowledge, capability and the people who have enhanced your life so far. Have the courage to look for the wisdom and mercy behind whatever hardship, setbacks and even injustices you have encountered in the past. In time, by the Grace of God you will find what you are looking for. Consider them as 'boot camps' or 'training sessions' you had to go through to become the resilient, compassionate and stronger person you are today.

You are an organic being. This opens up a mindset that helps you to grow as a person.

External connection gives you the perspective to view all encounters as 'tests' in life. By keeping the end in mind, it opens the pathway for you to connect with events and people in your life with a clear purpose. The purpose is for you to make effort, to deal with them in the best manner in seeking God's pleasure so you can return to your Creator with a clear conscience.

The practice of APCAR (Aware-Ponder-Connect-Act-Rectify/Review) process helps you to make better decisions. Practise BRAT (Breathe-Remember-Ask-Think Ihsan) in moments that test your patience. It can become a habit to not react in a way you may regret later. It is like the habit of stepping on the brake in an emergency situation when you are driving. Implementing the Guide enhances your wellbeing, by the will of God, both in this life and in the Hereafter. The rippling positive effect on your children by you modelling wellbeing practices in your life will In Shaa Allah (by the Will of God) be tremendous.

We are *parenteers*. We do not have all the answers. We need to rely on a map to get to our final destination. We do what we can for our children to the best we know. Outcomes are not in our hands. Do not obsess over the outcome. Focus only on our effort. This way, we continue to learn and grow with our children at every stage of their development. Each child will have his/her own path to travel. We walk with them part of their journey, and we help them search the best path forward for them. If we admit that we have no power or might and seek not to be left to our own devices for even the blink of an eye, wouldn't we teach our children to ask the same for themselves?

We are only trustees to our children for a time. We do not even know how long that trusteeship is! We need to remember that the paths we pursue are only testimony to our sincere efforts in fulfilling our trusteeship. We cannot guarantee the outcome; nor can any agent, from among creations who help our children, guarantee the outcome.

Behind the heartbreak and hardship is a plan we cannot foresee nor comprehend. Should the time come when we have to give them back before our departure from this life, we need to remember that we are handing them back to the One who will take care of them better than ourselves, while thanking the Lender for the opportunity for us to experience the kind of love like no other. We ask the One who guides to guide us all. We ask the One who bestows blessings to bless our efforts. We ask the One who heals to heal our pain. We ask not to be held responsible for the outcome. We seek forgiveness in our mistakes and shortcomings. We ask that our sincere effort in fulfilling our role as parents be accepted.

As Rais Bhuiyan aptly stated, 'Institutional education doesn't show you how to be polite, how to be compassionate, how to be a better human, unless your parents and teachers are willing to go the extra mile.' [174]

You have been charged with the task of raising another human being, the most honoured of creations. Every endeavour to do it well is a worthwhile pursuit. Let us join hands to go the extra mile for our children's wellbeing. Let this book be your companion that reminds you to water your own roots along this journey!

Glossary of Terms

'Aql: This is an Arabic term loosely translated as the reasoning or the mind. It is likened to the executive director of the Qalb. Whatever the Qalb wills the 'aql sends the order to the agencies such as the senses, limbs and tongue to carry out the will. However, in the Qur'an, this word never appears as a noun. It is always used in its various verb conjugations, which brings an extra dimension to the mind that is capable of exercising control or restraint. Scientists have identified this capability as a person's ability to delay gratification, to inhibit socially inappropriate behaviour or to sacrifice for a higher purpose.

Dhikr: A ritual of uttering remembrance of God performed in Arabic. The purpose of this ritual prayer is to glorify God and to seek greater spiritual connection.

Fitrah: Human beings are all born with a natural disposition of purity and innocence. Muslims believe that all human beings are born with Fitrah, having acknowledged God's Lordship and having made a covenant with God prior to being brought to the physical life on earth. This is the primordial nature of human beings.

Hadith: A collection of narrations from the sayings,

traditions, actions and tacit approval of Prophet Muhammad (peace and blessings be upon him). It is the second primary source of Islamic teachings after the Qur'an.

Hajj: This is the fifth pillar of Islam. It is the once in a lifetime pilgrimage to Makkah compulsory upon all adult Muslims who are mentally, physically and financially able. It involves fulfilment of several rituals across a number of fixed days in the twelfth month of the Islamic lunar calendar. Those who have the ability can perform this religious duty on someone else's behalf after he/she had performed their own Hajj previously. Muslims can perform Umrah (a voluntary pilgrimage) throughout the year outside the designated days for Hajj.

Iblees: This is the name of Satan who was from among the Jinns. Iblees is the one who made the first human being Adam, to slip up by his prompting. He and his followers are cursed and have been doomed to hell due to their insistence to disobey God out of their arrogance.

Jinn: This is the species name given to a type of creation, different from angels and humans. God informs us in the Qur'an that Jinns were created from smokeless fire. In this present world they are invisible to the human eye. They lead parallel lives to humans. Like humans, they have families and among them are some who believe and some who disbelieve in God. The good Jinns obey God and do not interfere with human life. The evil Jinns, collectively known as Satan, out of their defiance and contempt, vowed to do their level best to bring as many humans to Hell by way of whispering to the human's inciting nafs to commit all kinds of sins. Those who

Satan influences will have to face the consequences in the Hereafter, except those who repent and strive to reform to live by the commandment of God and teachings by God's messengers (peace be upon them all).

Naaseyat: This is a term in the Qur'an often translated as the forelock. In the Qur'an this part is associated with the descriptions of lying and sinning. Neuroscience research in recent years has identified this part of the brain, i.e. the frontal lobe of the brain, as the area where cognition, higher order thinking and synthesising of information are processed.

Nafs: Nafs is a word used in the Qur'an most commonly appearing as a noun. It is the entity that has been given the agency of free will in every person in the worldly life to choose between good and evil. Translations of the word nafs vary from author to author, including self, soul, personality or ego.

Nafs Al-Ammarah: It is a state of the nafs translated as the 'commanding nafs', the 'domineering nafs' or the 'self that incites to evil' by different authors. This is the aspect of the human soul that is inclined towards immediate gratification of lower desires, irrespective of the consequences or the means through which such pleasures are attained. An untamed nafs is easily influenced by his/her own lower desires and the promptings of Satan to evil.

Nafs Al-Lawwamah: This is a different state of the nafs from Nafs Al-Ammarah, translated as the 'reproaching nafs', the 'regretful nafs', or the 'blaming nafs' by different authors. This is the aspect of human soul with a conscience that feels regretful of one's sins or wrongdoings. When the rooh pulls the heart towards its Creator after the person has committed a sin, the soul becomes aware of the darkness from its wrongdoings and feels regretful and wishes to turn back to God, seeking forgiveness, mercy and guidance. Sometimes the Qalb knows what it desires is wrong, and the Qalb struggles in its decision between following Nafs Al-Ammarah and paying attention to nafs al-lawwamah.

Nafs Al-Mutmainnah: It is a state of tranquillity of the nafs translated as the 'nafs at peace', the 'tranquil nafs' or the 'serene nafs'. The traits of this state of the soul include generosity, contentment, surrender to God, pleased with whatever God decrees and seeking only to please God.

Qalb: This term means heart. It is also the spiritual heart where the nafs and rooh are housed. In Arabic it literally means change. Qalb is a noun with a distinct figurative attribute in Arabic as an entity that is constantly turning one way or another. The rooh is pulling the Qalb towards obeying God and yearns to return to God while the nafs is pulling the Qalb to the attractions of the physical world. Remembrance of God settles the Qalb. Repentance, charity, and good deeds purify the Qalb.

Qur'an: This is the divine speech of God revealed to Prophet Muhammad (peace and blessings be upon him) through the messenger, Arch Angel Jibreel (Gabriel). It is the final and complete revelation of God to mankind.

Rooh: Rooh is the human's individual pure spiritual being. Put it in another way, rooh is the element of human life. All rooh was created in Heaven before each person was brought to 'life' in their physical form on Earth at their appointed time. According to the Qur'anic teachings, all creations including human rooh acknowledged God's Lordship. Our rooh is the constant entity before, during and after our physical existence on Earth. Some translate the word rooh into soul or spirit. It is the human's divine essence that yearns to return to its Creator.

Sabr: Sabr means patience, steadfastness, perseverance in Arabic. It springs from a strong baseline of trust in the Divine decree and intervention.

Salat: A formal prayer with a routine of movements and recitations as taught by Prophet Muhammad (peace and blessings be upon him). It includes the five daily compulsory prayers at their specific time slots, recommended Sunnah prayers and voluntary prayers.

Satan: The Arabic pronunciation is Shay-taan. This is the term used for the evil Jinns.

Siyam: Siyam is the fourth pillar of Islam. It is a mandatory fast for a whole month observed by adult Muslims who are mentally and physically able. They exercise restraint from all prohibited actions and abstain from food, drink and sexual activities from the break of dawn until just after sunset. It is a yearly ritual that takes place in the ninth month of the Islamic lunar calendar by the name of Ramadan. Muslims undergo spiritual and physical cleansing during this month for 29 to 30 days (depending on moon sighting).

Sunnah: Sunnah is the body of customs, habits, words, decisions and practices of Muslims modelled by Prophet Muhammad (peace and blessings be upon him).

References

Chapter One

1 Mylittlemoppet, 'Parenting Quotes,' Pinterest, accessed June 29, 2020, in.pinterest.com/Mylittlemoppet/parenting-quotes/.
   William Edward Burghardt Du Bois, 1868-1963. African American sociologist, historian, civil rights activist, author, writer, and editor.

2 Mylittlemoppet, 'Parenting Quotes,' Pinterest, accessed June, 2020, in.pinterest.com/Mylittlemoppet/parenting-quotes/.
   Marisa de los Santos, American author and poet.

3 Barbara Fredrickson, *Positivity* (London: One World Publication, 2011), 21-24.

4 Drew DeSilver and David Masci, 'World's Muslim Population More Than You Might Think,' Pew Research Center, last modified January 31, 2017. http://pewresearch.org/fact-tank/2017/01/31/worlds-muslim-population-more-widespread-than-you-might-think/

Chapter Two

5 Qur'an 29:64, *The Qur'an: English Meaning and Notes* by Saheeh Internations.

6 Yasmeen Mogahed, *Reclaim Your Heart* (CA, USA: FB Publishing, 2012), 77.

7 As a sign of respect for all prophets, Muslims are enjoined to send salutations when any one of them is mentioned.

8 Qur'an, 4:1, trans. Abdel Haleem: 'People, be mindful of your Lord, who created you from a single soul, and from it created its mate, and from the pair of them spread countless men and women far and wide….'

9 Qur'an 15:29, by Saheeh International, Footnote number 632: 'The element of life and soul which Allah created for that body, not His own spirit or part of Himself (as some mistakenly believe).'

10 Abu Mustapha Al-Kanadi, *Mysteries of the Soul Expounded* (Birmingham: Al-Hidaayah Publishing and Distribution Ltd., 2003).

11 Muslim Central. 'Sajid Umar – Difference Between Nafs and Ruh.' YouTube video, 1:55. May 12, 2016. youtube.com/watch?v=VM4yPnDRXoE.

12 Qur'an 23:12-16, trans. Abdel Haleem.
'We created man from an essence of clay, then We placed him as a drop of fluid in a safe place, then We made that drop into a clinging form, and We made that form into a lump of flesh, and We made that lump into bones, and We clothed those bones with

flesh, and later We made him into other forms—Glory be to God, the best of creators!—then you will die and then, on the Day of Resurrection, you will be raised up again'.

13 Muhammad bin Ismail Al-Bukhari, *Sahih Al-Bukhari*, trans. Muhammad Muhsin Khan (no city: Dar Al-Fikr, no date), vol. 4, bk. 54, no. 430, 290-291.

14 Qur'an 19:35, trans. Abdel Haleem

15 Sean Martin, 'Life After Death: Scientists Reveal Shock Findings from Groundbreaking Study,' *The Express*, January 29, 2017, https://www.express.co.uk/news/science/670781/There-IS-life-after-DEATH-Scientists-reveal-shock-findings-from-groundbreaking-study.

16 Qur'an 6:60, trans. Abdel Haleem.

17 Said Nursi, *The Words*, trans. Huseyin Akarsu (New Jersey: The Light, 2005), 82.

18 Ibid, 94.

19 *Al-Bukhari*, vol. 6, bk. 60, no. 457.

20 Othman Aljilani, 'The Coccyx Miracle in Islam and Science,' trans. R. C., (research summary by Dr. Othman Aljilani in the 7th Conference of Scientific Miracles in the Koran and the Sunna, Dubai, 2004), accessed June 30, 2020 https://www.answering-christianity.com/coccyx_miracle.htm

21 Ibid.

22 Rachel Dodge et al., 'The challenge of defining

wellbeing,' *International Journal of Wellbeing* 2, no. 3 (2012): 222-235. doi:101.5502/ijw/v2i3.4

23 Martin Seligman, *Flourish* (New York: Atria, 2013), 237-241.

24 The National Wellness Institute, 'The Six Dimensions of Wellness,' The National Wellness Institute, accessed June 30, 2020. https://nationalwellness.org/resources/six-dimensions-of-wellness/#:~:text=Wellness%20is%20a%20conscious%2C%20self,Wellness%20is%20positive%20and%20affirming

25 Shawn Achor, *The Happiness Advantage* (London: Virgin Books, 2010).

26 Qur'an 26:88-89, trans. Abdel Haleem.

27 Ibid 76:3, 'We guided him to the right path, whether he was grateful or not.'

28 Muslim ibn al-Hajjaj, *Sahih Muslim*, transl. Abdul Hamid Siddiqui (Beirut: Dal Al Arabia, n.d.) vol. 4, no. 6418.
Abdullah b. 'Amr b. al-'As reported that he heard Allah's Messenger (may peace be upon him) as saying, '… O Allah, the Turner of hearts, turn our hearts to Thine obedience'.

29 The Qur'an 26:88-89, English Meanings and Notes by Saheeh International.

30 The Qur'an 13:28-29, trans. Abdel Haleem: 'those who have faith and whose hearts find peace in the remembrance of God—truly it is in the remembrance of God that hearts find peace—those who believe and

do righteous deeds: joy awaits these, and their final homecoming will be excellent.'

31 Emily Dickinson, 'Forever is Composed of Nows', Poetry Foundation, last accessed Jun. 30, 2020. https://www.poetryfoundation.org/poems/52202/forever-is-composed-of-nows-690. Emily Dickinson (1830-1886), American poet.

32 The Qur'an 2:286, trans. Abdel Haleem: 'Allah does not charge a soul except [with what is within] its capacity. It will have [the consequences of] what [good] it has gained, and it will bear [the consequences of] what [evil] it has earned.'

Chapter Three

33 Ibn Qayyim Al-Jawziyya, *Al-Fawa'id: A Collection of Wise Sayings*, trans. Bayan Translation Services (Al-Mansura, Egypt: Umm Al-Qura for Translation, Publishing and Distribution, 2004), 315

34 Paul T. P. Wong, 'Meaning in life,' In *Encyclopedia of Quality of Life and Well-being Research*, ed. by A. C. Michalos (New York, N.Y.: Springer, 2014), 3894-3898.

35 Stephen R. Covey, T*he 7 Habits of Highly Effective People* (New York: Fireside, 1989), 96-144.

36 Walter Mischel and Ebbe B. Ebbesen, 'Attention in Delay of Gratification,' *Journal of Personality and Social Psychology* 16, no. 2 (1970): 329-337. http://doi.org/10.1037/h0029815 .

37 Walter Mischel, Yuichi Shoda and Monica L. Rodriquez, 'Delay of Gratification in Children,'

Science 244, no. 4907 (1989): 933-938. Doi:10.1126/science.2658056

38 B. Resnick, The 'Marshmallow Test' Said Patience Was a Key to Success. A New Replication Tells us S'more,' *Vox*, Jun. 6, 2018. https://www.vox.com/science-and-health/2018/6/6/17413000/marshmallow-test-replication-mischel-psychology .

39 Ibn Qayyim Al-Jawziyya, *Al-Fawa'id: A Collection of Wise Sayings*, trans. Bayan Translation Services (Al-Mansura, Egypt: Umm Al-Qura for Translation, Publishing & Distribution, 2004), 318-319.

Chapter Four

40 Jalaluddin Rumi, *Selected Poems by Rumi*, translated and selected by Coleman Banks, (London: Penguin Books, 1995), 43. (Jalal ad-Din Muhammad Rumi was a Persian poet in the 13th-century. He was also a scholar in Islamic jurisprudence and theology)

41 Aminah Mah, 'Parenting Second Generation Muslim Australians: Living Islam to Achieve Success', MEd diss., (University of Western Australia, 2009).

42 Qur'an 16:96, trans. Abdel Haleem.

Chapter Five

43 Qur'an 3:112, trans. Abdel Haleem.

44 Abdallah Rothman and Adrian Coyle, 'Toward a Framework for Islamic Psychology and Psychotherapy: An Islamic Model of the Soul', *Journal of Religion and Health* 57, (15 June 2018), 1731-1744.

45 Ibid, 1736.

46 Abu Hamid Muhammad ibn Muhammad Al-Ghazali, *Ihya' 'Ulum-ud-Din: The Revival of Religious Learnings*, trans. Fazal-ul-Karim (Lahore: Kazi Publications, 1971), Vol. 3, p. 3.

47 Qur'an 12:53, trans. Abdel Haleem: 'I do not pretend to be blameless, for man's very soul incites him to evil unless my Lord shows mercy: He is most forgiving, most merciful.'

48 Qur'an 75:2, trans. Abdel Haleem: 'and by the self-reproaching soul!'

49 Ibid, 89:27-30, 'you soul at peace: return to your Lord well pleased and well pleasing; go in among my servants; and into My Garden.'

50 Ahmet Tanhan, 'Acceptance and Commitment Therapy with Ecological Systems Theory: Addressing Muslims Mental Health Issues and Wellbeing' *Journal of Positive Psychology and Wellbeing* 3, no. 2, (2019), 197-219.

51 Ibid, 207.

52 Rothman and Coyle, 1736.

53 Jamaal al-Din M. Zarabozo, *Purification of the Soul* (Denver, Colorado: Al-Basheer Company for Publications and Translations, 2002), 67.

54 Hisham Kabbani, 'Jihad Al Akbar' in Islamic Belief and Doctrine According to Ahl al-Sunna: A Repudiation of 'Salafi' Innovations, accessed April 20, 2018, sunnah.org/tasawwuf/jihad004.html

55 Qur'an 4:111; 7:177, trans. Abdel Haleem.

56 Robert Frager, *Heart, Self & Soul* (Wheaton, Illinois: Quest Books, 1999), 52.

57 Jamaal al-Din M. Zarabozo, *Purification of the Soul* (Denver, Colorado: Al-Basheer Company for Publications and Translations, 2002), 63.

58 Robert Frager, *Heart, Self & Soul*, 66.

59 Qur'an 89: 27-30, trans. Abdel Haleem.

60 Skellie, Walter James, The religious psychology of Al-Ghazzali: a translation of his book of the Ih'ya on the explanation of the wonders of the heart with introduction and notes, (Hartford: SN 1977), 6. PhD thesis (1938) University Microfilms International, Ann Arbor, Michigan. Hartford Seminary Foundation.

Chapter Six

61 Carl G. Jung, 'Approaching the Unconscious', in *Man and His Symbols*, edited by Carl G. Jung (Anchor Press: New York) 1964, 85

62 Facts & Statistics, Anxiety and Depression Association of America, ADAA. Information updated August 2017 http://about/adaa.org/press-room/facts-statistics .

63 www.mindmatters.edu.au/about-mindmatters/news/article/2016/05/05/anxiety-in-young-people

64 Telethon Kids Institute, Anxiety and Depression, https://www.telethonkids.org.au/our-research/

research-topics/anxiety-and-depression/ Accessed October 25, 2020

65 All translation of terms according to Walter James Skellie, The Religious Psychology of Al-Ghazzali: A Translation of his Book of the Ih'ya on the Explanation of the Wonders of the Heart with Introduction and Notes (Hartford: S.N., 1977). PhD thesis (1938) University Microfilms International, Ann Arbor, Michigan. Hartford Seminary Foundation.

66 Safiullah, M. M., *Into the Heart of Reality: The Inner Voice* (Bloomington, Indiana: Author House, 2013), 65.

67 Rothman and Coyle, 'Toward a Framework for Islamic Psychology ', 1736.

68 Anonymous, cited in Barbara Fredrickson, *Positivity* (London: One World Publication, 2011), 179.

69 Qur'an 7:172, trans. Abdel Haleem.

70 Muhammad bin Ismail Al-Bukhari, *Sahih Al-Bukhari*, trans. Muhammad Muhsin Khan (no city: Dar Al-Fikr, no date), vol. 4, bk.55, no.549, 346-347.

71 Qur'an 17: 85, trans. Abdel Haleem.

72 Shabnam Dharamsi and Abdullah Maynard, 'Islamic-based Interventions,' in *Counseling Muslims: Handbook of Mental Health Issues and Interventions*, eds. Sameera Ahmed and Mona M. Amer, (London: Routledge, 2012), 135-160.

73 An-Nawawi, *Forty Hadith*, trans. Ezzeddin Ibrahim

and Denys Johnson-Davies (Beirut, Lebanon: Dar Al-Koran Al-Kareem, 1976), Hadith 6, 42.

74   Walter James Skellie, The Religious Psychology of Al-Ghazali: A Translation of his Book of the Ih'ya on the Explanation of the Wonders of the Heart with Introduction and Notes (Hartford: S.N., 1977), 6. [PhD thesis (1938) University Microfilms International, Ann Arbor, Michigan. Hartford Seminary Foundation.]

75   Magharoui, Mokhtar. 'Episode 5—What is the heart?' YouTube video, 6:53, April 1, 2016 https://www.youtube.com/watch?v=qeRxId5f7o

76   Qur'an 95:4-8, trans. Abdel Haleem

77   Sunan Ibn Majah, no. 88 accessed July 24, 2020. ahadith.co.uk/permalink.php?id=6668

78   Al-Ghazali, Ihya', Vol. 3, 10-11.

79   Al Ghazali, Ihya' Vol. 3, 11

80   Sunan al-Tirmidhi, n. 2499. Hadith reported by Anas ibn Malik.

81   The Qur'an 87: 14-19, trans. Abdel Haleem.

82   Nazan Aksan and Grazyna Kochanska, 'Links Between Systems of Inhibition from Infancy to Preschool Years', *Child Development*, 75 (2004): 1477-1490.

83   Bryan W. Sohol, Stuart I. Hammond and Marvin W. Berkowitz, 'The Developmental Contours of Character', in *International Handbook on Values Education and Student Wellbeing*, ed.

Terence Lovat et al. (New York: Springer Science + Business Media B.V. 2010): 579-603. DOI: 10.1007/978-90-481-8675-4_33.

84 Ibid.

85 The Qur'an, 96:15-16, trans. Abdel Haleem: 'No! If he does not stop, We shall drag him by his forehead— his lying, sinful forehead.'

86 The Hans Wehr Dictionary of Modern Written Arabic, ed. J. Milton Cowan, 3rd ed. Ithaca, New York: Spoken Languages Services Inc., 1960), 3rd ed.

87 Alejandra Salazar, 'Frontal Lobe: Areas, Functions, and Disorders Related to it,' Mental, Physical Health and Neuroscience, *Cognifit*, June 13, 2017, https://blog.cognifit.com/frontal-lobe

88 At-Tirmidhi, no. 2140

89 Michael A. Ferguson et al., 'Reward, salience, and attentional networks are activated by religious experience in devout Mormons', *Social Neuroscience* 29 (Nov 2016): 8-9. http://dx.doi.org/10.1080/17470919.2016.1257437

90 Muhammad bin Ismail Al-Bukhari, *Sahih Al-Bukhari*, trans. Muhammad Muhsin Khan (no city: Dar Al-Fikr, no date), vol. 1, bk.1, no.1, 1.

91 'The Iceberg of Human Behaviour,' *Towerstone*, June 28, 2017 towerstone-global.com/iceberg-human-behaviour.

92 Sue Langley, CEO of The Langley Group, Diploma

of Positive Psychology and Wellbeing, March 3, 2016.

93 Qur'an, 2: 255, trans. Abdel Haleem: 'God, there is no god but Him, the Eve Living, the Ever Watchful. Neither slumber nor sleep overtakes Him. All that is in the heavens and in the earth belongs to Him. Who is there that can intercede with Him except by His leave? He knows what is before them and what is behind them, but they do not comprehend any of His knowledge except what He wills. His throne extends over the heavens and the earth; it does not weary Him to preserve them both. He is the Most High, the Tremendous.'

94 Qur'an, 112: 1-4, trans. Abdel Haleem: 'Say, 'He is God the One, God the eternal. He begot no one nor was He begotten. No one is comparable to Him.'

95 Liu Ji Rong, 'Wou Men Yao Bi Ci Ting Hua' (We should listen to each other [transl.]), *Tainengxinli-2002*, Issue 864, Oct 16, 2017, mp. weixin.qq.com

96 'Mindfulness,' Workbook, Diploma of Positive Psychology & Wellbeing (Sydney: The Langley Group, 2016) 10030NAT, 14.

97 Sonja Lyubomirsky, *The How of Happiness* (New York: Penguin Press, 2007), 20.

98 Ibid, 68.

99 Qur'an 66:6, trans. Abdel Haleem.

100 'Christopher K. Germer Quotes', Goodreads,

accessed July 29, 2020, https://www.goodreads.com/author/quotes/2849344.Christopher_K_Germer

101 Kristin Neff, 'Self-Compassion', accessed July 29, 2020, www.self-compassion.org

102 David Van Nuys, 'An Interview with Kristin Neff, Ph.D., on Self-Compassion', Wise Counsel podcast, Mentalhelp.net. Emotional Resilience, Jackson Hole Community Counseling Center, accessed July 29, 2020, https://www.jhccc.org/poc/view_doc.php?type=doc&id=43061

103 Marie Forleo, 'Elizabeth Gilbert & Marie Foleo on Fear, Authenticity and Big Magic', YouTube video, 47:57, published on 22 September, 2015, https://www.youtube.com/watch?v=HyUYa-BnjU8

104 David Van Nuys, 'An Interview with Kristin Neff, Ph.D., on Self-Compassion', Wise Counsel podcast, Mentalhelp.net. Emotional Resilience, Jackson Hole Community Counseling Center, accessed July 29, 2020, https://www.jhccc.org/poc/view_doc.php?type=doc&id=43061

105 TEDx Talks, 'The Space between Self-Compassion and Self-Esteem: Kristin Neff at TEDx CentennialParkWomen', YouTube video, 19:00, February 6, 2013, https://www.youtube.com/watch?v=IvtZBUSplr4

Chapter Seven

106 Walter James Skellie, The Religious Psychology of Al-Ghazali: A Translation of his Book of the Ih'ya on the Explanation of the Wonders of the Heart with

Introduction and Notes (Hartford: S.N., 1977), 203, note no. 35. [PhD thesis (1938) University Microfilms International, Ann Arbor, Michigan. Hartford Seminary Foundation.]

107 Qur'an 2:32, trans. Abdel Haleem.

108 Raindrop Academy, 'My Personal Transformation', LaunchGood, July 29, 2020, https://www.launchgood.com/project/raindrop_academy

109 Qur'an 6:103, trans. Abdel Haleem.

110 https://www.drhappy.com.au/

111 Tim Sharp, Newsletter 31 July, 2017, paragraph 3, The Happiness Institute & Dr Happy.

112 Stephen R. Covey, *The 7 Habits of Highly Effective People* (New York: Fireside, 1989), 80.

113 China Liaoning Official TV Channel. 'Story of Dai, Bin-Ling in Wan Mei Gao Bai' (Open Declaration [transl.]). YouTube video, 50:01. Published January 17, 2017. https://www.youtube.com/watch?v=Ph9W5L1ubak

114 An-Nawawi, *Forty Hadith*, trans Ezzeddin Ibrahim and Denys Johnson-Davies (Beirut: Dar Al-Koran Al-Kareem, 1976), Hadith no. 13, 56.

115 Safiullah M. M., *Into the Heart of Reality: The Inner Voice* (Bloomington, Indiana: Author House, 2013), 71.

116 Qur'an 3:137, trans. Abdel Haleem: 'God's ways have operated before your time: travel through

the land, and see what was the end of those who disbelieved?'

117 Qur'an 26:62, trans. Abdel Haleem.

118 Muslim ibn al-Hajjaj, *Sahih Muslim,* trans. 'Abdul Hamid Siddiqi (Beirut, Lebanon: Dal Al Arabia, 1971), 4:2076.

119 Safiullah M. M., *Into the Heart of Reality: The Inner Voice* (Bloomington, Indiana: Author House, 2013), 51.

120 Qur'an 31:22, trans. Abdel Haleem

121 http://www.telegraph.co.uk/news/uknews/crime/9785714/Devoted-mother-beat-son-to-death-for-failing-to-learn-Koran.html

122 Sue Roffey, *Circle Solutions for Student Wellbeing* (London: Sage, 2014), 2nd ed.

123 Ibid, 3.

124 Ibid, 5.

Chapter Eight

125 Dyer, Wayne W. 'Success secrets'. The official Wayne Dyer blog https://www.drwaynedyer.com/blog/success-secrets/

126 Hadith, *Fortress of the Muslims*, complied by Sa'id bin Wahf Al-Qahtani (Riyadh: Darrusalam, 2009), 109.

'O, Ever Living One, O Eternal One, by Your mercy I call on You to set right all my affairs. Do not place me in charge of my soul even for the blinking of an eye.'

127 Wenlei Ma, 'Incredible Couple's Story Immortalised on Screen', News.com.au December 20, 2017, https://www.news.com.au/entertainment/movies/new-movies/incredible-couples-story-immortalised-on-screen/news-story/0a166a7398b2865f15a3ae3f9b932c1d

128 Ibn Al-Qayyim Al-Jawziyya, Ibn Qayyim Al-Jawziyya Quotes, AZ Quotes, accessed May 15, 2017, https://www.azquotes.com/author/28408-Ibn_Qayyim_Al_Jawziyya

129 Ibn Katheer, *Stories of the Prophets*, trans. S. Gad, T. Abu As-Su'ood & M. A. M. Abu Sheisha (El-Mansoura, Egypt: Dal Al-Manarah).

130 Ibid.

131 Qur'an, 21:83-84, trans. Abdel Haleem.

132 Sophia, B. J. Liu, *Ling Jie De Yi Zhe* [Interpreter of the spiritual realm] (Taipei: Suncolor, 2017).

133 Muslim ibn al-Hajjaj, *Sahih Muslim*, trans. 'Abdul Hamid Siddiqi (Beirut, Lebanon: Dal Al Arabia, 1971), no. 2996.
Prophet Muhammad (peace and blessings be upon him) said, 'The angels are created from light, the jinn are created from smokeless fire, and Adam was created from that which has been described to you.'

134 Abu Zakariya Yahya bin Sharaf An-Nawawi, *Riyadh-us-Saleheen*, trans. S. M. Madni Abbasi (Karachi, Pakistan: International Islamic Publishers Ltd., 1983), chapter. 247, no. 1447.

135 Qur'an, 72:1-15, trans. Abdel Haleem.

136 Ibid. 2:34: 'When We told the angels, 'Bow down before Adam,' they all bowed. But not Iblees, who refused and was arrogant: he was disobedient.'

137 Ibid. 15: 32-50: 'God said, 'Iblees, why did you not bow down like the others?' and he answered, 'I will not bow to a mortal You created from dried clay, formed from dark mud.' 'Get out of here!' said God. 'You are an outcast, rejected until the Day when they are raised from the dead.' 'You have respite,' said God, 'until the Day of the Appointed Time.' Iblees then said to God, 'Because You have put me in the wrong, I will lure mankind on earth and put them in the wrong, all except Your devoted servants.' God said, '[Devotion] is a straight path to Me: you will have no power over My servants, only over the ones who go astray and follow you. Hell is the promised place for all these, with seven gates, each gate having its allotted share of them. But the righteous will be in Gardens with springs—'Enter them in peace and safety!'—and We shall remove any bitterness from their hearts: [they will be like] brothers sitting on couches, face to face. No weariness will ever touch them there, nor will they ever be expelled.' [Prophet], tell My servants that I am the Forgiving, the Merciful, but My torment is the truly painful one.'

138 Qur'an 2:155-157, trans. Abdel Haleem.

139 '19 Eye-opening Rumi Quotes for Navigating the Maze of Life,' Book Retreats, quote no. 8, accessed July 29, 2018, https://bookretreats.com/blog/19-eye-opening-rumi-quotes-for-navigating-the-maze-of-life/

140 Hadith, *Fortress of the Muslims*, complied by Sa'id bin Wahf Al-Qahtani (Riyadh: Darrusalam, 2009), 158.

141 Qur'an 18:46, trans. Abdel Haleem.

142 Stephen R. Covey, *The 7 Habits of Highly Effective People* (New York: Fireside, 1989), 71.

143 The Montessori Method, 'Maria Montessori Quotes,' American Montessori Society, accessed August 3, 2020, https://amshq.org/About-Montessori/History-of-Montessori/Who-Was-Maria-Montessori/Maria-Montessori-Quotes

144 www.abc.net.au/abcforkids/shows

145 Qur'an, 2:126-129, trans. Abdel Haleem: 'Abraham said, 'My Lord, make this land secure and provide with produce those of its people who believe in God and the Last Day.' God said, 'As for those who disbelieve, I will grant them enjoyment for a short while and then subject them to the torment of the Fire—an evil destination.' As Abraham and Ishmael built up the foundations of the House [they prayed], 'Our Lord, accept [this] from us. You are the All Hearing, All Knowing. Our Lord, make us devoted to You; make our descendants into a community devoted to You. Show us how to worship and accept our repentance, for You are the Ever Relenting, the Most Merciful. Our Lord, make a messenger of their own rise up from among them, to recite Your revelations to them, teach them the Scripture and wisdom, and purify them: You have the power to decide."

Chapter Nine

146 Safiullah, M. M., *Into the Heart of Reality: The Inner Voice*, (Bloomington, Indiana: Author House, 2013), 78

147 Abdul Wahid Hamid, *Companions of the Prophet*, (Leicester, UK: MELS, 1995), vol. 1, 103-110.

148 An-Nawawi, *Forty Hadith*, trans Ezzeddin Ibrahim and Denys Johnson-Davies (Beirut: Dar Al-Koran Al-Kareem, 1976), no. 13, 56.

149 Aaleen, 30 May 2018, Culture. Accessed July 9, 2018 https://www.786cosmetics.com/this-mans-story-will-change-your-life-ali-banat/.

150 https://www.onepathnetwork.com/gifted-with-cancer/ November 16, 2015. Accessed July 9, 2018.

151 Rais Bhuiyan's TED talk. https://www.youtube.com/watch?v=v4uEVdGoBik Published 10 Aug 2017. Accessed 9 July 2018.

152 Nicole Brodeur, 28 July 2017. Seattle Times. https://www.seattletimes.com/entertainment/books/after-being-shot-in-the-face-rais-bhuiyan-becomes-forgiveness-ambassador/ accessed 9 July 2018

Chapter Ten

153 Ibn Qayyim Al-Jawziyya, *Provisions of the Afterlife*, trans. Ismail Abdus Salaam (Beirut: Dar Al-Kotob, Al-ilmiyah, 2010), 647

154 Qur'an 3:200, trans. Abdel Haleem.

155 Qur'an 31:17, trans. Abdel Haleem.

156 John Gottman, *Raising an Emotionally Intelligent Child* (New York: Simon & Shuster Paperbacks, 1977), Chapter 2, 42-68

157 Ibn Qayyimg al-Jawziyya, *Patience & Gratitude*, 2nd ed. (Al-Mansura, Egypt: Umm Al-Qura for Translation, Publishing & Distribution, 2002), 22.

158 Qur'an, 64:15, trans. Abdel Haleem.

159 Angela Duckworth, author of Grit: The Power of Passion and Perseverance. www.goodreads.com/work/quotes/45670634-grit-passion-perseverance-and-the-science-of-success

160 https://www.catholic.org/news/national/story.php?id=75295

161 Julia Long, 'Pornography is more than sexual fantasy. It's cultural violence.' *Washington Post*. May 28, 2016. https://www.washingtonpost.com/news/in-theory/wp/2016/05/27/pornography-is-more-than-just-sexual-fantasy-its-cultural-violence/?noredirect=on&utm_term=.984bcbb9d21f

162 Qur'an, 2:153, trans. Abdul Haleem.

163 Story of Moses and the man who was granted mercy and knowledge. The Qur'an 18:66-82

164 Qur'an 67:1-2, trans. Abdel Haleem.

165 Sufiullah, M. M., *Into the Heart of Reality: The Inner Voice*, (Bloomington, Indiana: Author House, 2013) Footnote 44, 38.

166 Qur'an, 64:15-16, trans Abdul Haleem.

167 Muhammad ibn Ismail Al-Bukhari, *Sahih Al-Bukhari*, trans Muhammad Muhsin Khan (Beirut: Dar Al-Fikr, n.d.) vol. 2, bk. 23, no. 372.

168 Qur'an, Chapter 12: Yusuf.

169 Muhammad bin Ismail Al-Bukhari, *Sahih Al-Bukhari*, trans. Muhammad Muhsin Khan (Beirut: Dar Al-Fikr, no date), vol. 7, bk. 70, no. 545, 371-372.

170 Qur'an, 6:59 'He has the keys to the unseen: no one knows them but Him. He knows all that is in the land and sea. No leaf falls without His knowledge, nor is there a single grain in the darkness of the earth, or anything, fresh or withered, that is not written in a clear Record.'

171 Hadith Tirmidhi, 47: 3527, Muflihun, accessed August 11, 2020 https://muflihun.com/tirmidhi/47/3527

172 Ibid, 47: 3515.

173 Sunan Ibn Majah 3846, 'Hadith on Dua: Ask Allah for Pardon and Wellness', Abu Amina Elias, accessed August 11, 2020 https://abuaminaelias.com/dailyhadithonline/2019/06/08/dua-ask-afwa-afiyah-akhirah/

174 https://www.seattletimes.com/entertainment/books/after-being-shot-in-the-face-rais-bhuiyan-becomes-forgiveness-ambassador/

About the Author

Born in Taiwan, Aminah received her secondary school education in Malaysia, then furthered her studies in Australia where she settled eventually. Aminah's passion in wellbeing has been shaped since her late teens by both her nursing and education backgrounds. Her years of experience working with the Muslim communities in Sydney and Perth as well as her teaching endeavours extended her academic interests in parenting and wellbeing research which earned her both a Masters and a PhD degree in Education from the University of Western Australia. In 2017, Aminah gained a Diploma in Positive Psychology and Wellbeing. Due to Aminah's husband's work commitments, she frequently travelled between Saudi Arabia and Australia to be in the company of her husband and three children. Since 2019, Aminah became the proprietor of her handmade natural skincare business, Dewtiful Natural Skincare. Travel restrictions as a result of COVID-19 in 2020 opened the way for Aminah to take part in wellbeing development and youth education programs.

CONNECT WITH THE AUTHOR ONLINE

info@dewtiful.com.au

www.dewtiful.com.au

www.instagram.com/naturally_dewtiful

www.ingramcontent.com/pod-product-compliance
Lightning Source LLC
Chambersburg PA
CBHW050305010526
44107CB00055B/2114